PRAISE FOR
ALL THINGS RECONSIDERED

"It has been my great luck to find Knox McCoy. His effortless, on-the-spot humor, while making me seethe with envy, absolutely translates to the page in *All Things Reconsidered*. In this book, you will find masterful storytelling, relatable humanity, and an unexpected story about picking up Cheesy Gorditas from Taco Bell in the drive-through with a naked friend. I'm just saying there is a lot in here, all hilarious and surprisingly tender. Knox is an American treasure."

—Jen Hatmaker
Author of *Fierce, Free, and Full of Fire: The Guide to Being Glorious You*

"In a world that worships certainty, Knox McCoy invites us to give our first impressions a second look and reconsider what we thought we knew for sure. With grace-filled humility, hard-won wisdom, and just the right amount of ridicule, Knox's writing continues to challenge, entertain, and influence the way we talk about what we believe. I adore this book, and I hope Knox continues to write books forever. This statement needs no reconsideration."

—Emily P. Freeman
Wall Street Journal bestselling author of *The Next Right Thing*

"In *All Things Reconsidered*, Knox McCoy is engaging and imaginative as he paves the way for the rest of us to examine, and perhaps question, long-held ideas that no longer represent how we think, what we believe, or how we feel. In a fast-paced culture like ours, this is the reminder we need if we are to contribute our own thoughtful, creative, and sometimes new ideas to the larger conversation."

—Suzanne Stabile
Author of *The Path Between Us* and coauthor of *The Road Back to You*

"Entertaining, thought-provoking, and laugh-out-loud funny. Knox McCoy writes the books Chuck Klosterman would write if he'd grown up going to Sunday school."

—Chad Alan Gibbs
Author of *Two Like Me and You*

"We live in an age that villainizes changing your mind. Knox is here to reclaim the lost art of reconsideration. He is a thoughtful captain: helping you navigate the shallow coastlines and subterranean waters of the sacred and the secular, with equal weight and precision to each. Release yourself from the stigma of stubborn and inflexible beliefs and allow yourself to consider again, with Knox as your guide and *All Things Reconsidered* as your map."

—Erin Moon
Author of *Every Broken Thing: A Lent and Holy Week Guide to Answering Ecclesiastes*

"In his thoughtful new work, a 'celebration of recalibration,' Knox McCoy manages once again to unite comedy and candor, penning serious reflections that are seriously funny. His reflections on introversion and the Enneagram had me in tears, I was laughing so hard."

—Anne Bogel
Author of *Don't Overthink It* and *I'd Rather Be Reading*

"This is the perfect book at the perfect time. For people weary of the us-versus-them culture, Knox offers smart, funny, and thoughtful permission to reconsider our lives with a kind posture, exemplifying how we can do the same for our own people."

—Kendra Adachi
Author of *The Lazy Genius Way*

ALL
THINGS
RECONSIDERED

ALSO BY KNOX MCCOY

*The Wondering Years: How Pop Culture Helped
Me Answer Life's Biggest Questions*

ALL THINGS

RECONSIDERED

HOW RETHINKING WHAT WE KNOW
HELPS US KNOW WHAT WE BELIEVE

KNOX MCCOY

W PUBLISHING GROUP

AN IMPRINT OF THOMAS NELSON

Published in Nashville, Tennessee, by W Publishing, an imprint of Thomas Nelson.

The author is represented by Alive Literary Agency, 7680 Goddard Street, Suite 200, Colorado Springs, Colorado 80920, www.aliveliterary.com.

Thomas Nelson titles may be purchased in bulk for educational, business, fundraising, or sales promotional use. For information, please email SpecialMarkets@ThomasNelson.com.

Any internet addresses, phone numbers, or company or product information printed in this book are offered as a resource and are not intended in any way to be or to imply an endorsement by Thomas Nelson, nor does Thomas Nelson vouch for the existence, content, or services of these sites, phone numbers, companies, or products beyond the life of this book.

ISBN 978-0-7852-2096-1 (eBook)
ISBN 978-0-7852-2092-3 (TP)

Library of Congress Cataloging-in-Publication Data

Library of Congress Control Number: 2020932716

Printed in the United States of America

20 21 22 23 24   LSC   10 9 8 7 6 5 4 3 2 1

To Ashley, the best of wives and best of women

CONTENTS

CONTENTS

PART THREE: RECONSIDER BELIEFS

FOREWORD

When Knox asked me to write this foreword, I immediately said yes. Then I read his book. (Spoiler alert: it's fantastic and I would pay cash money for it.) Then I googled "how to write a foreword."[1] What I found were several writerly sites that indicate forewords are not necessary. This felt like a personal attack. So I clicked on page 2 of the search results. These sites were much more pro-foreword and therefore more trustworthy. The consensus seemed to be that an author should choose someone who is an expert in the field the book is about and who can offer his or her credibility to the project.

I have a bachelor's degree in reconsideration. Technically, my degree is in "sociology and women's studies," which is why my father thinks I have a weird job as a podcaster, but *no matter*. I've spent most of my days assured I know exactly how I feel about things and then completely changing my mind later.

- I knew I would never watch a show as good as *Saved by the Bell*. Then I watched *30 Rock*.

---

1. To be completely transparent, I first googled "how to write a forward," which is not what this is. Although in my defense, this is in the forward part of the book sometimes known as the front. I'm a great writer.

- I believed Chris Hemsworth was the hottest Chris. It is obviously Chris Pine.
- I thought I looked stunning with bangs, then I saw pictures of myself with bangs.

Knox has been a huge contributor to my reconsideration efforts. He and I met in an online writing forum in 2011. I considered anyone in an internet writing forum to be pretentious.[2] When I visited Knox's website, the most recent post on his blog was a three-thousand-word masterpiece recapping the latest episode of *The Bachelor*. I instantly reconsidered my take on online writers.

In 2013, Knox asked me to cohost a podcast with him. I thought podcasters were boring middle-aged nerds who interviewed other nerds as a hobby. We started *The Popcast*, a show about pop culture that is now our current day job. I learned that podcasters are actually *very pretty* and *interesting* and *young*.

It's not just my opinions about writing and podcasting that have changed. Knox convinced me Shia LaBeouf is a great artist. *The Peanut Butter Falcon* and *Honey Boy* proved his case. After several post–live show trips to McDonald's, I thought twice about who makes the best chicken nuggets.[3] Knox has made me reconsider character-driven novels, Danny McBride, the value of multiple whiteboards, and owning a business with someone you met in a writing forum.

The most recent frontier of Knox's influence on me has been regarding faith. I grew up going to church every Sunday, but I believed God was a bit of a tyrant; God himself showed me

---

2. Not me. I was only pretentious about the pretentious people.
3. It's McDonald's. Seriously.

repeatedly that he is kind and good. From that goodness, Knox and I launched a podcast called *The Bible Binge* where we recap stories in Scripture as though they were movies or TV shows. We cast the characters with current celebrities, and our staff Bible scholar rebukes any glaring theological mistakes we might make. In our first episode on Adam and Eve, Knox innocently turned and asked me, "What part of this story do you think is an allegory?"

My longtime legalist heart started beating fast at the idea that Knox might suggest the Bible isn't an ironclad official historical record. I raised my voice and responded with a stern "NONE OF IT. IT IS PERFECT AND CORRECT AND IT ALL HAPPENED." He didn't argue back or roll his eyes or try to change my mind. He simply moved on to the next task at hand. But that exchange planted a seed. Not a pause in doubt but a seed of reconsideration. That reconsideration hasn't driven me away from God, but it's plunged me further into his Word and my relationship with him.

Knox is curious yet faithful. He is questioning yet believing. His kind inquiries have guided me through second looks at Harry Potter, hot sauce, and even the holy Word of God. Let Knox show you how reconsideration has transformed his thoughts on everything from the silly to the serious, and perhaps it will plant a seed in you too.[4]

—Jamie Golden

---

4. Stop it. This is a metaphor about farming and how farmers plant seeds and then we get trees that make books, ET CETERA. Reconsider farming and trees and your mind, you sicko.

INTRODUCTION

Consider this hypothetical: You have a dog. You love this dog and are emotionally, spiritually, and familially invested in this dog. You feed it and, in return, it barks at strange noises outside the house. Your relationship is a partnership with a fondness bordering on love.

But then one day you walk in the door from work and the dog greets you with his tail wagging, except this time he's holding a crossbow. Not with his mouth. He's holding it with his paws (you know, in the way dogs can manipulate things with their paws). And somehow this beloved canine of yours has manipulated the crossbow to point directly at you. His tail continues wagging, but suddenly you aren't sure whether he's being playful or threatening. And what's more, at this moment you experience a realization: you don't even own a crossbow.

How do you react?

Do you now recognize this dog as an adversary? Or do you see this scene as a compilation of several bizarre micro-coincidences that led to your dog holding you at crossbow-point?

The rational part of your brain considers the situation and surmises that what's going on is most likely serendipitous. While there have certainly been stories where dogs accidentally discharged guns, have you ever in your life read about a dog not just firing a gun but also premeditating everything in the lead-up to that moment? I haven't—and trust me, if I had, I would remember something like that.

However confident you are in this being coincidence over betrayal, the instinctual part of your brain can't help but react to the crossbow pointed at your face. And remember the tail wagging? I can't emphasize how unsettling something like that would be.

Even though everything you've learned in life has reinforced the idea that a dog, besides being literally man's best friend, cannot intentionally use a firearm or crossbow with intent to kill, in the moment, you reconsider this reality. Because, well, you kind of have to.

Originally I had a completely different idea for this book. It wasn't going to be about reconsiderations or dogs with crossbows or most anything else now contained within these pages. I still may eventually use the original idea, so I won't say too much about it—but my agent liked it. My wife, Ashley, liked it. Most importantly, I super liked it.[1]

But then some happenings happened, and that original idea wasn't possible. And so, on February 17, 2019, I woke up at 3:00 a.m. with a new deadline and a writing future to reconsider.

I did what any writer does when faced with an imminent deadline: I browsed Instagram. Really just for inspiration (and by "inspiration," I mean distraction).

---

1. The idea was fine. I'm making it sound like I wrote *The Godfather: Part IV* or something. Settle down, Introduction Knox.

I was looking for anything that wasn't a book idea, and eventually I made a vague but cathartic post on Instagram about how I was starting from scratch on a new idea. Killer Instagram content, I know. Very relatable and not at all melodramatic.

Later on, a friend messaged me some encouragement, and among the encouragement was this advice: "Don't try to create it; try to find it."

Which, I have to admit, made no sense to me. That sounded like the kind of fortune-cookie message that gets wait-listed. But the more I thought about these words, the more they spoke to me in a helpful way.

The great misconception around writing a book is that it's an act of creation[2] in which you are just communicating the things you already know and feel. In truth, a lot of writing is about discovery. Discovery about what you want to say, sure, but more discovery about what you think. And this discovery extends beyond writers and books.

Look, we're living in a time of absolute inundation. Every day we're bombarded with information, interactions, and notifications all vying for our attention. Just a generalized consideration of all these things is a herculean task. Forget actually digging into each stimulus to see the larger and more substantive implications it carries.

Like, right now, in this very moment, I feel the end of the world could be imminent, but I do not know from what. It could be white supremacists, White Claw drinks, climate change, a new

---

2. I'm currently obsessed with *Hamilton*, so lyrics from the soundtrack are definitely going to creep into this book. When that happens, I want to recognize them. This is a very self-indulgent thing, but I'm a self-indulgent person, so I'm not throwing away my shot (OMG, do you get it?) at intertwining these passions, and you are just going to have to deal with it.

version of Thanos, Russia, Taylor Swift, or any number of other threats foreign and/or domestic. I can recognize all of these elements as threats, but I don't have time to understand them. I want to, truly I do, but I also have fifty-nine kajillion other things I have to process, so my attention is a hundred miles long but only one centimeter deep. And this is the issue I'm getting at: we are losing the important ability to deeply comprehend.

The price of this conclusive expediency is that we're tasked with understanding something fully and completely as soon as we're introduced to it. But as we know, modern events and ideas are complicated, and we don't always see the full picture immediately. Once we do see the full picture, it may reveal that our initial assumptions were incorrect, like when I saw the trailer for Adam Sandler's *Little Nicky* and predicted that it would be one of the greatest comedy movies ever.[3]

Or seeing the full picture may confirm that our first instinct was the right one all along.

Accordingly, this book is a celebration of reconsideration. Some of the things talked about in these chapters are small and inconsequential, while others are much larger and existential. It's important for me to clarify the following, though: this isn't a life-coach book where I dispense vague notions of how to be.[4]

This book isn't the definitive rendering of what is true and untrue in the world. Please read that again and again. I have no degrees, no expertise, and no fancy résumé plumage that should intimidate you into taking what I say and believing it to be the

---

3. This did not happen. Not even a little.
4. *Not a Life-Coach Book Where I Dispense Vague Notions of How to Be* is what I wanted as the title for this book, but my editors called that title option "cumbersome," "plainly moronic," and "an overall terrible idea."

metaphysical and ultimate truth for all time forever and ever, infinity, no takebacks.

But this book *is* very much a celebration of the power of reconsideration as seen through the prism of things I've reconsidered, as this process helped me more fully articulate what I believe and why.

It is my belief that we're currently in the middle of a cultural overdose on authenticity—but without that necessary companion of vulnerability. I love that we're all being so authentic and genuine. But to me, the best connections come when we pair that authenticity of thoughts, feelings, and beliefs with the vulnerability of why we believe them. I hope this book will be a window that allows you to do the same in your own life, whether a crossbow-wielding dog is involved or not.

HOW TO READ THIS BOOK

So, look, in a lot of ways this may be a weird read.

First off, it's not fiction. So it's already not like other books because it's not *The Girl Next Door's Husband's Wife in Cabin 32 Who Went Missing and May Be Dead or Dying*. I do apologize that this book isn't that, but I will try to conjure up some mysterious elements when I can.

As you probably already know, this book is nonfiction. Although it's not nonfiction in the sense that it's about some cool historical event like the fall of the Roman Empire or whether Bradley Cooper and Lady Gaga hooked up on the set of *A Star Is Born*.[1]

This book isn't even a self-help book. I mean, I try to assist you in some way, but not in a very forward-facing way. I've read a ton of books that tell you exactly what to do, when to do it, how to do it, and when to stop apologizing for it, but this book isn't going to be like that.

Instead, it's just a transparent account of my pursuit to better understand various topics and ideas for myself.

You are obviously free to agree with, disagree with, or be

---

1. You guys, they obviously did. C'mon.

enthusiastically indifferent about my conclusions. But bigger than what those exact conclusions end up being, the hope is that reading about my journey of reconsideration will provoke some aftershocks of reconsiderations in your own life wherever you may need them.

I've always been much more interested in *why* people think and believe what they do as opposed to the contents of the beliefs. The why is infinitely more fascinating to me, as it contains an entire universe of experiences that help me not just understand a belief but also empathize with it.

Given that, my biggest hope for this book is not that you would walk away believing and supporting every conclusion I've drawn for myself but rather that it spurs you on to figure out what you think for yourself and why.

PART ONE

RECONSIDER SELF

It now seemed to me that all my other guesses had been only self-pleasing dreams spun out of my wishes, but now I was awake.

—C. S. LEWIS, *TILL WE HAVE FACES*

ONE

WHEATFIELD WITH CROWS

I remember the first time I was blindsided by the idea of reconsideration. I was a senior in high school, and my AP English teacher, Mr. Lambert, gave us an exam that required us to react to a piece of art. I know that probably sounds like I went to school in a place that only exists in the world of *Big Little Lies*, but I can assure you that my high school was accredited. Mr. Lambert was the best teacher I'd ever had, so when he presented the idea, most of us in the class bought in immediately. As I've gotten older, I've found that the better you are at something, the more you can experiment with the form of things, and that's what Mr. Lambert was doing with us.[1]

The piece of art in question was Van Gogh's *Wheatfield with Crows*, which, if I could, I would include here so you could experience a similar exercise. It's a beautiful and vivid piece of art with vibrantly yellow wheat juxtaposed against an ominously darkened sky dotted and complicated with the presence of toucans flying through it. Just kidding. It's dotted with the presence of

---

1. This axiom clearly explains the career of Kanye West.

crows, obviously; thus the name. But seriously, how great would a brooding, moody piece of art be with just a metric butt-ton of Toucan Sams?[2] *Wheatfield with Toucan Sams*? I'm officially commissioning someone to do this.

Anyway, our midterm was this: write five hundred or so words on what feelings this picture provoked. It seemed simple enough. I dutifully interpreted away and consulted my emotions in order to provide a high-minded essay about something I wasn't really that invested in. I know you and I don't know each other, but I'm not someone who has a ton of emotional or intellectual proximity to crows or wheat fields.

After we turned in our pages, Mr. Lambert gave us a new assignment. It was the same request as before (write what emotions and feelings the *Wheatfield with Crows* piece evoked), but he added context that we hadn't considered the first time around: the reality that this picture was the last thing Van Gogh painted before committing suicide.

I remember absorbing this information and being absolutely electrified, for several reasons.

First, the exercise's creativity was off the charts. I also think this happened around the same time I first saw *The Sixth Sense*, so I was very much into the plot-twistification of movies leaking into my daily life.

Second, this was yet another reminder about how much cooler English class was than any math class ever, and I will fight you if you feel differently.

Third, this was the most demonstrative example I'd ever seen about how useless our initial perceptions can be.

---

2. As in, Toucan Sam, the mascot of Froot Loops. If you needed this footnote to explain that, I'm not mad at you, but I am disappointed.

Now, I was aware how deeply rooted truths can evolve. For example, I'd lived most of my life thinking that DC Talk was the best music group in the history of the world. But eventually I made the transition into realizing that the best music group in the world was actually a tie between P.O.D. and Creed.[3]

Bad music taste and a penchant for hyperbole aside, it wasn't that I didn't believe those things; it was just that things changed. It doesn't mean I didn't hold those opinions, but my experiences and opinions evolved once I was exposed to different kinds of music.

Similarly, with *Wheatfield with Crows*, not knowing about its context in Van Gogh's life made it just a picture to me, no different from *The Starry Night* or a comic from *The Far Side*; it was just a collection of line squiggles and artistic flourishes designed to evoke something untethered from real life.

But once Mr. Lambert made me aware that this picture was incredibly tethered to real life, how could that context not suddenly be the most important thing about the picture? Instead of seeing just line squiggles and artistic flourishes, you could make the case that this picture was a cry for help, a suicide note, both, or neither. But regardless of where you land, clearly this contextualization demands a reconsideration of the initial assumption.

I think there's a bit of a negative specter when it comes to reconsidering your assumptions. To me, this has a lot to do with the soft oppression of low expectations, as in, "I know enough; what more do I need?" Or even, "I skimmed the headline/article/book, and I pretty much have the gist of it."

But just as I experienced with the painting, "enough" means

---

3. I wish this was a joke, but it's just biographical.

a very different thing than "complete." Not that we can ever completely understand everything everywhere all the time, but perhaps we should challenge ourselves to consistently seek a more complete picture.

As a senior in high school, I couldn't definitively say what Van Gogh was thinking and what this piece of art meant. Years later I still can't, but my appreciation of the painting grew more complete as I learned more context.

And that's what I love about reconsideration. Too often we give real estate to things in our lives that either haven't earned their land or were never meant to occupy important space in the first place. I say this as someone who not only is part of a generation who finds reassessment difficult amid all the available distractions but also has a front-row seat to a parade of developments all but demanding our reappraisal:

- The political system is in tatters as partisanship holds democracy hostage, leading us to wonder what a political identity truly means.
- The US banking system almost submarined the global economy and mostly got off with a slap on the wrist, leading us to wonder if we can trust an institution we assumed to be objective.
- American school shootings are at an epidemic level, and yet no legislation has been introduced to even reasonably curb their occurrence, leading us to wonder what it will take for our country to consider gun reform.
- Our weather and environments are growing increasingly more unstable, leading us to wonder what humanity's massive population means for the future of the planet.

It's asking a lot for us to process these problems. While our impulse is to oversimplify or blame them on our ideological opposites, the reality is that these are big and complicated issues involving significant nuance.

As with *Wheatfield with Crows*, it's no longer enough to just react to an issue or idea before moving on. It's our obligation to dig a little deeper to more completely understand it.

TWO

BOY, CHANGE YOUR FACE

I have an okay face. I'm mostly content with it. I mean, I'm not throwing a parade for it or anything, but I'm basically okay with how it all turned out. Could it have been better? Oh yeah, most definitely. It's a little jowly, and I have this weird scar on the left side of the bridge of my nose even though I've never been hit or pox-afflicted precisely there, but whatever. There are worse faces, there are better faces, and mine is nestled in the central somewhere of mostly mediocre faces.

The reason I'm thinking about this is because I'm faced (nailed it) with a reality that involves having more photos of me taken than I would naturally select for myself. And when you are in more photos than usual, you also tend to scrutinize yourself more than usual. Does that make me a narcissist or just an average person? I think there's a thin line between being appropriately concerned with your appearance and becoming Mariah Carey, but if not wanting to look like a swamp monster in pictures makes me a narcissist, then stock my dressing room with blue peanut butter M&M's only, because I'm fine with it.

9

I'll explain this uptick in photo frequency in a moment, but first you should know that this photographic reticence is mostly because the secret of looking great in a photo is kind of a foreign language to me, and the stakes of taking a bad photo are now higher than ever.

It used to be that candid pictures were snapped almost exclusively for rarely-looked-at coffee-table photo books. But now they're for the entire internet, where all your social media and real friends are able to scrutinize your photo to get a better sense of whether you've been doing the Whole30 diet or the Whole 30 Oreos diet.

Also, apparently there's a geometry to being photographed well? Like you have to create angles with your arms? I wasn't told that there would be math involved, so I'll consider this development the revenge of high school algebra and geometry teachers.

Lastly, I'm learning that you have to be mindful of lighting. Although I have to say that while good lighting is an idea I understand to exist, if given $10,000 and twelve hours to identify it, I don't believe I could do so. Not to brag, but I have a bit of a superpower in the form of always being able to find lighting that makes me look like I'm taking a mug shot. So that's nice.

Now that you sense my anxiety about having my photo taken, I will explain why it happens so frequently. There's been this weird development with my job where I'm required to be more visible. You would think that getting into the podcast game would mean that you're safe from concerns about how your face looks, but for *The Popcast with Knox and Jamie*, we managed to complicate this by scheduling events where we not only do our podcast for a live audience but also hang out with listeners afterward. Although at first this was incredibly intimidating for an introvert like me, it's turned into one of my most favorite things, because we get to put names to faces and spend time with people who spend time with our show.

And in most of these post-show interactions, the natural move is to take a picture, because we all do things mostly for the gram, your boy here included. Which is when the hijinks ensue.

Let me say this: I'm not an awkward person. I know that totally sounds like something an awkward person says, but let me qualify that statement. I'm not saying that I'm completely immune from moments of spontaneous awkwardness. No way, friendo; it's quite the opposite. I can be aggressively awkward if the conditions are right. In *Jurassic Park*, Jeff Goldblum taught us that life finds a way, but for me, so does awkwardness.

But on a larger level, when my soul is weighed at the end of my life, I feel very confident that it will bear out that awkwardness wasn't my default setting a majority of the time. Now, it might be a 51–49 situation, but a majority is a majority, you know?

Anyway, when we first started the routine of taking post-live show pictures, this unfortunate cloud of awkwardness would just take hold of me. All decorum and normal human conduct went straight out the window. You ever see *Talladega Nights: The Ballad of Ricky Bobby*? There is a scene when Will Ferrell's Ricky Bobby is interviewed after a race, and he doesn't know what to do with his hands while he's talking. That was pretty much me in these post-show pictures. I was constantly confused and confounded[1] by these situations. One show I just clenched my fists like I was an *Arthur* meme. In another, I held my arms out directly perpendicular to my body like I was Jack from *Titanic*.

---

1. *Hamilton* reference.

Also, the issue of my face. So many laments for my face.

This is the problem when you don't have a ton of picture-taking reps under your belt. You never have a natural sense of comfort with how you should look.

My goal in pictures was to look as skinny as possible; I was aiming for a 100-percent-pure-yield skinniness. But the complicated nature of achieving this ambition usually just turned me into a photographic Icarus flying way too close to the sun,[2] and I ended up looking like a human form of the Ghostface mask from the *Scream* movies. I truly do not understand what happened in these pictures.

The more live shows we did, the more pictures I took, which seemed helpful because I could find my baseline normal-face smile. Unfortunately, I took all these extra opportunities to experiment more in an effort to achieve Best Case Scenario–Looking Knox. Sadly, in my pursuit of facial excellence, I was making the entire process too complicated. In some pictures I would let my face go slack and thrust out my neck like a newly unhibernated turtle. In others I would open my mouth wide but drop my chin as if the timing of this photo coincided with the most natural and authentic guffaw of laughter that there had ever been. In yet others I would open my eyes very wide like someone who had just seen a ghost, or I would squint my eyes like someone who was bird-watching. (Because I assume bird-watchers squint a lot? But they always have binoculars, don't they? Never mind—I squinted like people who squint for a specific and humorous reason.)

Clearly, there was an issue.

---

2. *Hamilton* reference.

But then my wife introduced me to the "smize." This move, originated by Tyra Banks, is the art of smiling with your eyes, which even now I don't fully understand. How do you smile with your eyes? Don't you just see with your eyes? And if you are smiling with your eyes, what is your mouth supposed to be doing? It's all so mystical.

But the smize as I understood it involves a concerted effort to look unconcerned, and therein lies the richer intellectual text for us to consider.

See, pictures are intimidating for me because there's an on-the-recordness to them that you can't mitigate. And for someone like me, this is constraining. Pictures are so definitive, and my tendency is to run from the obstruction of absolute definitiveness. There's so much to know and learn—why get preoccupied with locking something in when you can continue to learn and understand something more deeply? At least that's the charitable interpretation I allow myself.

More realistically, my reluctance is about avoidance. Why take a picture now when we can take it in the future when I've been given time to look better? Instead of confronting exactly what I look like now, I'd rather just kick that can down the road to allow myself to lose twenty pounds and miraculously develop a jawline that someone could carve granite on.

I consider myself a reasonable and rational person, yet I consistently apply this Schrödinger's cat-ification to my life: If I never see the bad thing, does it really exist?

I've had times where I avoided looking at my bank account because I worried what the number might be—a momentary respite that in no way helped the problem and, in most situations, made it much worse. As it turns out, avoiding the necessity of handling your financial situation[3] is not a savvy personal finance strategy.

Even as a professional on-the-internet person, I avoid looking at the feedback for things I work on because that's my way of leveraging control. And though I know that often what I dream up in my imagination is worse than reality, this fear of criticism keeps me from the joy of accomplishment or encouragement.

But even more (and this might be a societal curse that our age is uniquely afflicted with), I think our access to connection and information can paralyze us with all the possibilities about what could be.

I tend to reconsider an action or idea so much that I get addicted to intellectual nomadism. It's more fun to be distracted by the possibilities than to commit to any one thing. I convince myself that the pursuit is pure and worthy because I'm seeking out the most optimum thing. But I think I just fall in love with the perpetual fluidity, which is very powerful because it keeps me from having to marry myself to specificity—and the good and bad that come with it.

There comes a point with all things—my finances, my work, or even my face—when I just have to stare them down to see them as they are. It may be as uncomfortable as looking at your face too long in the mirror or not knowing how to hold your arms in a picture, but these failures are the things we have to stare at in order to grow.

---

3. *Hamilton* reference.

THREE

PRONUNCIATIONS

Look, words are hard. Especially so now that we live in an age when we talk less and type more.[1] We don't get the verbal reps needed to hear how to say words out loud and in front of other people, but that doesn't mean it hurts any less to screw up the pronunciation of a commonly understood word in front of a crowd.

What follows is a collection of words and names I've historically mispronounced or continue to mispronounce.

- **Theater:** "Thee-eight-her"

    I tend to draw out words to add infinitely more syllables than are appropriate.
- **Chloe:** "Shlow"

    This is from the *Left Behind* series. When I read this name, which belongs to the daughter of the main character, Rayford, I'd never before seen such a confederation of consonants and vowels. "Shlow" was my best effort.

---

1. *Hamilton* reference.

- **D'Artagnan from** *The Three Musketeers*:
"Dee-art-UH-gannon"
    I felt really good about my guess, and—real talk—I'm 45 percent sure that I now know how to say this correctly.
- **Epitome:** "Eep-a-toem"
    What can I say? I've always respected *e*'s with a long vowel sound.
- **Zendaya:** "Zen-die-o"
    I cannot even explain where the *o* sound comes from. It makes no phonetic sense, yet here we are.
- **Appalachia:** "Appall-LAKE-ea"
    The proper pronunciation seemed quite an indulgence for a place not often described as fanciful.
- **Sprite:** "Spry-ought"
    I don't know why I say it like this. It took thirty-four years for me to be corrected on it, though.
- **Entendre:** "In-ten-dre"
    I still don't know that I'm completely aware of how to properly say this word, so I just go out of my way to avoid it.
- **Beignet:** "Beige-net"
    I should have known better, but I pronounced it like that because it looks like that. Fight me, but I'm not wrong.
- **Facade:** "Fay-KADE"
    This is one of those words where it took me a long time to realize that the word I was reading was the same word I heard properly pronounced.
- **Acronym:** "Ack-ro-knee-umm"
    Again, I have Extra Syllable Addition Disorder. What do you want from me?
- **Superlative:** "SUPER-lay-teev"

In sixth grade I mispronounced this while reading a chapter aloud in class. My teacher, Mrs. Stewart, launched into a detailed explanation about my mistake—an explanation I did not listen to. When prompted to begin again, I re-mispronounced the word. Mrs. Stewart was not amused.

- **Lagniappe:** "Lagkneeopee"

  I don't even feel bad. How could I possibly be expected to understand how to say this word?

- **Europe:** "Ee-uro-pee"

  I always respect the *e*'s to a fault. I told you that.

- **Bon Iver:** "Bone Iver"

  I whiffed on the "Bon" part, sure, but I feel like the last name is so open to interpretation that it's a little misleading.

- **Melancholy:** "Melon-cho-lee"

  It just seems like the waste of an *h* to have it there but not allude to it in the pronunciation.

- **Ashton Kutcher:** "Ashton CUT-chair"

  I also work way too hard to say his wife's name, Mila Kunis. I get the "Mila" part correct, but I suddenly go Brazilian with her last name: "Koo-knee-ice."

- **Reese's Pieces:** "REE-SEES PEE-SEES"

  This was installed deep into my consciousness from youth. It's just so close to a rhyme that the heart wants what it wants.

- **Fajita:** "Fah-JAI-ta"

  Look, when you are young and learning a new language, you don't know the nuances of when to apply a cultural pronunciation and when not to. My only regret was in the faces of my parents, who were briefly unsure whether I'd just misspoken or said a weirdly sexualized word.

- **Bourgeoisie:** "Boor-geo-esee"

  I don't feel bad about this one because there are seven vowels to four consonants. We're really off the letter grid, so whatever happens at that point happens.

- **Quinoa:** "Kwee-Noah"

  The thing about the *u* within the *q* orbit is that I always feel bad for it because it has to always be there but it never gets to shine. I like to think that this was my attempt to let the *u* live a little.

- **Gnocchi:** "Guh-know-key"

  Hand to God in heaven, I tried and failed at saying this seven days ago. You're never too old for words to be hard.

FOUR

WHAT IF I DON'T WANT
TO BE AN INTROVERT?

(WARNING: If you are easily triggered or annoyed by Enneagram talk, you might want to do a skiparoo on this chapter.)

Is it weird to say that for most of my life, from childhood until just a few months ago, I felt like one-half Donald Duck and one-half Mickey Mouse? Allow me to explain.

There's always been something about both Mickey and Donald that I related to but could never fully put my finger on, at least until I started thinking more about personalities.

The idea that both characters could be representative of me might be strange given that they are so vividly different, but the more you really look at these two, the more you realize that they are similar.

For example, each has an alliterative, patterned name (Proper Name / Animal). Each has a love interest with this same alliterative naming pattern (Minnie Mouse / Daisy Duck). These love interests also partner together in a hair bow accessory business.[1] A peripheral detail, but one we must consider.

Most interestingly, both are anthropomorphized by wearing clothes, which isn't really notable on its own, but it is notable when you realize that both are only half-dressed. Mickey wears only red shorts with yellow buttons and no shirt, while Donald wears only a sailor shirt and hat with no shorts. Even more, Mickey's iconic ears stand in stark contrast to Donald's complete lack of them.

What are we to make of this cartoon clothing complementarianism?

In terms of my own existence, I'm a dyed-in-the-wool introvert. I consider eye contact with strangers to be brazenly inappropriate, and I will go to incredible lengths to avoid small talk.

Even as I type these words, I sit in a Barnes & Noble coffee bar next to someone who, I feel pretty confident in saying, is trying to talk to me. Only moments ago, he sat down in the coffee bar. He lasted all of forty-five seconds before standing back up and approaching me to ask for a pen, which I gave him. When I did, he volunteered that it was for a very interesting book he was reading, and when he said "very" he infused it with so much mystery that it almost manifested the spirit of Hercules Poirot.

But as a savvy introvert, I can differentiate between someone wanting to connect over a truly great story and an extrovert just trying to vampire energy out of a random interaction. Thus, I

---

1. True to hierarchical form, the business is called Minnie's Bow-tique. Would it have killed Minnie to call it Minnie and Daisy's Bow-tique?

kept my headphones on, ignored the bait, and mouthed, "That's great" with a respectful thumbs-up before returning my attention to these very words. (Also, I should confess that my headphones aren't even playing music. I wear them mostly to discourage extroverts.) I truly do want the book to be great for him, but not so great that we must conversate about it. Why ruin a good thing?

Generally speaking, I like being an introvert, but I don't know how much that matters. I just kind of *am* an introvert, so I have to have a natural degree of fondness for something hard-wired into my essence. It's impossible to separate how much of my affinity for introversion is just confirmation bias and to what extent I just see it as objectively the preferable way to go about life.

In Enneagram speak I'm a five, which is called the Investigator. Investigators love learning, and we prize information, objectivity, and solitude, as all these help us feel competent and self-reliant. When you mock up the idea of an introvert in your head, we're a pretty close approximation of that cliché.

But weirdly, an Enneagram five also comes with this bizarre break-glass-in-case-of-emergency ability to shape-shift into an extrovert during times of stress. You can get really "through the looking glass" on this stuff if you want, but what this means is that I become a seven.

And if you know anything about sevens, they are not at all like fives. I realize that we're kind of Enneagram-ceptioning here, so let me try to simplify this conversation in terms you can understand even if you are not Suzanne Stabile or Beth McCord.

Imagine if Poppy from the *Trolls* movies were a real-life person. She's basically a seven. I'm extra familiar with this personality type because it's also the personality of my business partner, Jamie Golden.

When Jamie walks through a room, there's a literal wake of extroversion trailing her. It's like King Midas turning things to gold, except Jamie turns people into extroverts. Do you have someone in your life who, if you take them with you to renew your driver's license, leaves having been invited to five weddings and asked to become the godmother to multiple children they just met? That's Jamie.

She's the fun, the party, the mojo—which is exactly counter to everything I am.[2] Remember the anecdote I just told you about me conversation-blocking the guy wanting to talk about his book? Jamie would have started a book club with him right then.

So how does it make sense that my personality type can morph into hers in times of stress? Frankly, I have no idea. If you want to understand the Enneagram more, you should be reading a book about the Enneagram and not this one.

But I'd be lying if I said that I didn't love when this evolution happens. Because for a lot of what I do, extroversion would be a better fit.

I'm suited for writing as an introvert, true, but as a performer, both on podcasts (*The Popcast with Knox and Jamie* and *The Bible Binge*) and in live-audience settings, being an introvert with limited energy resources is very *mucho no bueno*.

Have you ever seen one of those horror movie scenes where someone walks into a jungle river only to find it infested with piranhas? You get the shot of that person in the water, and all these piranhas start taking tiny bites until all that's left is a hat or a shoe. That's what every day feels like for an Enneagram five.

---

2. If you wanted to compare me to Branch from *Trolls*, it wouldn't be unwarranted.

Every situation, interaction, and obligation takes little pieces of us until all that is left is a metaphorical hat or shoe.

And when that energy is gone, you can't really paddle-shock it back, because it's over. Our energy, our ability to process information or act like a basic, average human being, is gone. And I hate this aspect of my personality. It causes me great shame. Primarily because I feel emotionally incompetent and weak, and also because my worldview was shaped by wanting to emulate my father at every turn. I know I'm testing fate by introducing another Enneagram type here, but YOLO; he's a three, which means he's an Achiever. I wanted to be like him, to prize success, ambition, and achievement.

What do you do when you are fundamentally at odds with the essence of who you are and who you feel compelled to be?

Sometimes, when I'm away from home and in a setting and situation I'll never return to, I'll put on the guise of someone else. Not a different name or identity, but the countenance of an extrovert. I'll force myself to be bubbly and personable. I'll seek out eye contact and conversation just to see if my experience is different. And it always is. I always enjoy who I am outwardly much more, and the more I do it, the easier it gets. But it never stops feeling like I'm skydiving without a parachute, and also I'm on fire. As much as I want to evolve beyond myself, it appears that I'm fundamentally capped.

So I try to finesse the issue. When necessary, I take caffeine pills. Not to the extent that Jessie Spano did during her infamous breakdown on *Saved by the Bell*, but at a significant enough rate that it levels me up out of being who I most naturally am. And I'd be lying if I said I don't rely too much on alcohol sometimes to both provoke enthusiasm and soothe the emptied-out reservoirs.

In case you sense that I'm building up to a larger point about how you just have to hang in there and do the right thing and it will all work out, that's not happening. I'm not building to any big reveal of how I can handle this situation because I haven't found that solution yet. I don't know how to not rely on those things because I don't know how else to get the result I want. I see here on the page that this probably isn't the healthiest course. But what should also come through on the page is just how much I don't want to be limited like I am.

This feels like the right time to double back to Donald Duck and Mickey Mouse. Both as a child and as a parent, it's always been apparent to me that Donald resents Mickey. How could he not? They are mostly equals, except that Mickey is an icon and Donald is mostly his inelegant, inarticulate, and easy-to-anger foil.

But I realize now that Donald isn't resentful of Mickey; he's a necessity *for* Mickey.

For Mickey to be who he is requires a cast of personalities that tease out who we know him to be, and Donald Duck is the most preeminent of all these personalities because of how closely he matches Mickey in biographical detail.

Mickey wouldn't be Mickey without the presence of Donald, and Donald isn't Donald without Mickey. To fundamentally alter that arrangement would collapse the whole thing.

Similarly, as much as I want to force-evolve myself into someone with the best elements of my introversion along with the cherry-picked elements of the types I covet, it can't happen because that's not how our personalities function. The Enneagram doesn't work like that. To fundamentally change how I interact with the world and my motivation for living within it is to fundamentally change me—not just who I am, but *how* I am.

There's a tendency when you talk about personality types to distill everyone to his or her most simplified essence, and usually that essence is the fatal flaw of each personality type. While that's handy when you are trying to thumbnail-sketch people, it's wildly unfair because it discredits our complexity.

The point of the Enneagram (and personality tests in general) isn't to exist as a monument to self or an avenue to a pithy anecdote for get-togethers; it's about the acquisition of self-knowledge, which we can use to help make the world a better place.

The reconsideration here isn't about changing anything; after all, our wiring is our wiring. While we can evolve beyond our initial impulses to rely on the synopsis of ourselves (and our weaknesses), on a molecular level we have no opportunity to rebrand or reboot into another type or number.

But we can revise how we reconcile these truths. We can look at the core of who we are (e.g., an Enneagram five) and what we are not (e.g., extroverted and of limitless energy) and lament our limits or incompatibility with what we personally value. Or, like Mickey and Donald, we can meditate on how these things are true, how they are compatible, and how these unique gifts and talents allow us to influence the world for good.

FIVE

GOING TOO HARD IN
A SCHOOL PLAY

In sixth grade I was cast as the Wizard in our school's produc-
tion of *The Wizard of Oz*. This was my first theatrical role of
significance since first grade, when I'd let the entire school down
after forgetting the words to my solo for the song "Wonderful
Counselor." No one on the faculty told me that I'd let them down,
but I could always see it in their eyes.

From the second grade through fifth, I was exiled to the elementary school equivalent of Elba: just stagehand stuff here and
nonspeaking landscape characters there.

But I caught a break in sixth grade. In *Game of Thrones*,
Littlefinger memorably quipped, "Chaos is a ladder,"[1] and this was
absolutely true for me. After some faculty turnover, the institutional memory of my failure had been wiped clean. Accordingly,
I managed to grab a foothold of possibility in the form of being

---

1. *Game of Thrones*, season 3, episode 6, "The Climb," directed by Alik Sakharov, written
by George R. R. Martin, David Benioff, and D. B. Weiss, aired May 5, 2013, on HBO.

cast as Egeus in Shakespeare's *A Midsummer Night's Dream*. I say "foothold" because, if you know anything about this play, you know that Egeus is as crucial to *A Midsummer Night's Dream* as Hawkeye's archery skills were to beating Thanos. Nevertheless, I competently and stoically spoke my one line on stage, forgetting nothing, and in doing so, I shed the label of theatrical pariah I'd worn since first grade.

In the spring I parlayed my electric performance as Egeus into getting cast as the Wizard. It wasn't the Scarecrow or the Cowardly Lion or the Tin Man, but those parts had songs to perform, and I knew that asking myself to act *and* sing after the events of my first-grade failure was tempting fate, so I was over the moon about being the Wizard.

Knowing I needed to make up for lost time, I intended to really heighten and broaden my portrayal of the Wizard. Think Daniel Plainview from *There Will Be Blood* spliced with Tony Montana from *Scarface*. I consistently received acting notes from my teachers asking me to turn down the intensity, and while my external response was to always respectfully receive these notes, my internal response was pretty much, "It's called acting, sweetie. Ever heard of it?"

On opening night I was incredibly nervous but also intellectually zeroed in. I knew my script inside and out; there would be no forgotten words on my watch. Things went pretty well in the early part of the play, and we were approaching my favorite scene of the whole performance: me as the Wizard but disguised as the gatekeeper to the Emerald City. Dorothy and friends arrive and try to gain entry, and initially, I do not allow them in. But once she reveals her ruby slippers, my intended line is, "Well, bust my buttons, why didn't you say so in the first place? C'mon in."

In rehearsals I'd managed to turn this one line into a scenery-chewing expedition of actorly enthusiasm, and on the night of the performance, my intention was no different. But the execution was another story. Right in the middle of the crescendo of "Well, bust my buttons," my voice aggressively cracked so hard that it almost opened a rift in the space-time continuum. It's one thing for a voice to crack, but it's an entirely different thing for your voice to crack in front of an audience, especially in that pubescently trademarked way. You know what I'm talking about. The kind of crack that makes it excruciatingly obvious to everyone that you are actively navigating the ascent to masculinity by way of body hair, a patchy peach fuzz mustache, and frequent voice crackings.

I trailed the rest of my line off quietly and quickly, another casualty of the reality that we don't hit puberty—puberty hits us.

I've never forgotten this embarrassing experience, partly because that's how social trauma works; it becomes a part of who you are, destined to erratically flash into your consciousness at inopportune times, thereby submarining your confidence and sense of self like the *Titanic* post-iceberg.[2]

But I've also never forgotten because I can still feel the neediness that went into me trying to be the most theatrical and overwhelmingly entertaining Wizard of Oz to ever wizard in the land of Oz or any other fictional place.

---

2. Also because my friends who were there still frequently taunt me with this memory.

That neediness was so palpable, and it was infused with not just the need to be good but the need to be so good that it invalidated my current flaws and previous failures.

And that's the thing I learned to reconsider: stop keeping score with yourself. When you constantly keep score, you're never going to win. It's an elongated exercise in futility because (1) we're imperfect and (2) if you're like me, you hold on to the failures much longer than the successes. One hundred kind reviews about my writing are undone by a single harsh one.

I vividly remember crying tears of blinding rage when I failed at gym class kickball, and I still have scars on my knuckles from punching fences, walls, and dugout doors after failed plate appearances in baseball. The anger and rage that went into those tears and bloody knuckles were fueled by disappointment—not necessarily at the result itself but at my inability to engineer it to be what I wanted.

The essence of the disconnect between my anger and my failures is about being unable to direct my behavior toward the *purpose* of the task because I'm fixated on the *motivation* for the task. I'm constantly motivated not by the thing I'm doing but by the fear of not being competent.

To descend even more below the surface of my psyche, I'm motivated most of all by any insult, underestimation, or gesture of disrespect that has preceded the task. In fact, the inciting event of me writing my first book was a prominent internet person firing me from a gig under very shady circumstances.

Did I want to write books? Of course. That desire has been in me my entire life. But the thing that most pushed me to begin seriously writing was my anger and wanting to stick it to this person who did me wrong. And if you aren't immediately intuiting how insane this is, please take a minute and ruminate on the deeper psychological issues I clearly have.[3]

I know this feels like I'm angling toward a paragraph where I flip my self-destructive ways around and communicate how your flaws make you who you are, and that is so good and healthy, and you shouldn't apologize for it. But I think that is simultaneously very true and very untrue. Who you are often explains how you are, but that doesn't mean it's healthy.

As writers, we love to put a glossy spin on things and delicately shoehorn pithy anecdotes into a greater emotional or spiritual truth. There are many chapters in this book where I've intended to do that exact thing. (Never forget—most of all, writers are shameless manipulators.)

But sometimes there is no clean and pithy way to spin something into a distinctive truth. I probably should talk to a therapist about the deeper issues causing me to seek out disrespect in order to propel and inspire myself forward.

Why do I like being yelled at?

Why do I like to stand in the ocean and be crushed by large waves?

Why do I run in the heat wearing sweat suits?

There's clearly a posture of me inviting difficulty so as to provoke a specific response, but what is at the root of that impulse? I'm dying to know, but I'm also dying to not know.

Because if I ever do know, what if the ambition I can draw from this weird tension leaves too?

What if in solving myself I also solve whatever lack I'm

---

3. This is probably a bad time to mention that I keep a burn book of collected anecdotes in my office from when people have insulted or slighted me.

feeling that originates my ambition? I'm not saying I like who I am, but I also don't know who I am without those things.

It's murky and complicated, but it's a murky and complicated I am familiar with. There's a homishness to it that I've come to find comfort in, and—in the words of Dorothy Gale—there's no place like home.

SIX

FRIENDSHIP

A clichéd reading of a person with my specific personality type would conclude that I'm a bad friend, but nothing could be further from the truth. I'm actually a really good friend. I'm intensely loyal, I give good counsel and advice, and (weirdly) I love helping people move. Two of these three things are pretty great, especially the one about helping people move. The problem is that I'm a really difficult friend to make. Not because there's anything special going on but because I'm an introvert. I should say that it's easy for introverts to write themselves off as some kind of relational unicorn that is just waiting to be discovered and domesticated into friendship by someone special—but really, we're just socially obtuse. There's nothing majestic about it.

I take the friendships I do have very seriously and treat them with the utmost respect. But when those relationships get complicated, I'm cursed with an almost sociopathic ability to just concede them to the ether, which is why I've had multiple relationships break badly, followed by years of radio silence. But remember, I'm weirdly enthusiastic about helping people move, so it basically evens out.

Allow me to paint a vivid picture of this contentious dynamic using a situation from my freshman year of college.

After an adolescence built on the assumption that I would continue playing baseball for the entirety of my adult life before disappearing into Iowa cornfields like the characters in *Field of Dreams*,[1] I quit. I cannot overstate how big a deal this was. It was during a time when I deeply believed *Bull Durham*, *Little Big League*, and *Angels in the Outfield* were among the top-ten greatest films ever produced. Read that sentence again. My love for baseball was an infestation that extended to every cell of my being.

As for why I stopped playing, it was a complicated stew of reasons. First, I'd been playing baseball in the fall, spring, and summer since I was nine. I craved some seasonal freedom when I wasn't hitting soft toss and practicing outfield-to-infield relay protocol. Second, if I was going to make some changes, entering college seemed the time to do it. Third, and perhaps the realest reason, I couldn't hit a slider. Fastballs I had no problem with, and curveballs were doable. Changeups were a pain, but I could kind of cope with them. Sliders though? Not happening. On an infinite scale, scientists say that every iteration of every possible thing eventually happens, except for me hitting a slider. That one, they concede, will never happen.

So I left for Samford University in Birmingham, Alabama, and I made plans to room with my best friend from high school, Scott.*[2] We'd played baseball together, and we were both making

---

1. This is a thirty-year-old movie reference, but if you know, then you know.
2. I know I put an asterisk to make you think that wasn't his real name, but Scott is actually his real name, and I'm using it only because he loves any attention, be it good or bad.

the transition from baseball obsession to life beyond the dugout,[3] so it made sense to us to do that together. It wasn't necessarily that Scott and I looked at the dynamics of living together in a small room and felt we would be a great fit. We just knew we were friends, we were going to the same college, and the alternative to not rooming together was random drawing for our roommate designations.

To be super honest, for an introvert, the prospect of leaving your college roommate up to chance is so fabulously steeped in stupidity that I almost cannot take it. It's the emotional equivalent of attempting to shoot a half-dozen bottle rockets out of your butt. The downside is private part annihilation, and the upside is that there is no upside. If you take nothing else away from this book, remember that there is no upside to shooting a firework out of a bodily orifice, and there is no upside to randomness for a college roommate.

College admissions boards, you can swear up and down that you utilize an advanced algorithm (LOL) to make sure you pair up people with hypercompatible worldviews and personalities, but this is just an elaborate ruse. I'm supposed to place the future of my living quarters in the hands of a university that can't figure out parking or a cohesive intramural schedule? Imma pass on that.

Luckily for me, Scott and I were compatible enough. As I mentioned, we'd played baseball together, we held similar values, and we were both still in relationships with our high school sweethearts (who, incidentally, would go on to become our wives). In other words, while rooming together might not have been the

---

3. *Life Beyond the Dugout* sounds like the absolute worst memoir title from a former baseball player who uses baseball advice as a metaphor for life advice: "When stress has a full count on you, sometimes you just need to choke up on the bat of life."

superest, bestest bet given that both of us were emergent butterflies originating from sheltered cocoons, it certainly seemed like a safer bet than the other options.

Cut to four months later.

I won't assign blame, because I'm the author of this story, and it would be easy to cast Scott as the antagonist and me as the innocent victim. What's more likely is that Scott and I were both a-holes that year as we adjusted to a very different life that was not buoyed by parents, sports, church, and school. The decisions we made manifested our personalities in grotesque and malignant ways, culminating in an altercation late in our first semester.

For context, Scott, the extrovert, was prelaw, the freshman class president, and pledging Sigma Nu something. Conversely, I was the introvert and an English major, and the collegiate routine I developed was going to class alone, studying alone, reading in the dining hall alone, and running for exercise alone. Can you sense a trend?

This trend is one of the reasons my year at Samford was one of the most formative in my life. It functioned as the introvert pressure valve I never knew I'd needed or had the space to pursue. This was the year I started going to movies alone. Do you know how much of a pariah you think you should feel like when you go to movies alone in college? But for me it was glorious.

Occasionally I'd dip my toes into the socializing pool, which typically resulted in my one other friend, "The Ferg," and I playing *Madden 2001*. Because we were in a dorm room and seating was limited, I would secure permission from Scott to borrow his desk chair for The Ferg to sit in. Consider this chair Chekhov's Desk Chair.

One fateful day The Ferg and I were playing a particularly

intense game of *Madden*. Despite our having Scott's permission to use the chair, he returned to the room and demanded it back.

Since we were in the fourth quarter, I thought it was reasonable for Scott to let us finish the game with The Ferg utilizing Scott's chair. Scott disagreed on this point, so he attempted to pull my chair out from under me. I lightly and respectfully held him at bay with one hand, my other still on the controller.

However, things escalated quickly when Scott responded to my light stiff-arm in a way that did not feel remotely commensurate with what I was doing: he sucker punched me right in the ear. We're talking a knuckle-to-eardrum, *Mortal Kombat* "Finish him!" punch.

Have you ever been punched in the ear? It's a terrible place to get punched for a multitude of reasons:

1. Getting punched in the head just sucks in general. That's the place where you keep your brain, which is the real pilot of this flesh machine we call a body.[4]
2. There's something about how your ears affect your equilibrium that makes you feel like you're on a capsizing cruise ship when your ear gets punched. And not a classy cruise ship like the *Titanic*; a white-trash one where Kid Rock is judging a wet T-shirt contest while "Bawitdaba" plays at an ear-bleeding volume.
3. You literally see stars like in the cartoons.

Now you might be thinking, "But, Knox, is there really a *good* place to get punched? Isn't it bad across the board to get punched anywhere?"

---

4. Honestly, have you ever realized that we're all, essentially, like Krang from *Teenage Mutant Ninja Turtles*? It's true.

The answer to that misguided and incredibly simplistic question is that there's a whole spectrum of places where you can get punched, ranging from "not a big deal" to "as tragic as the dinosaur extinction."

- **The arm:** Primo punching real estate. It doesn't really hurt, *and* you get the added benefit of an awesome arm bruise, which makes you feel like Sly Stallone in *Over the Top* when he's required to arm-wrestle to win a real life for himself and his estranged son.[5]
- **The butt:** There's so much padding here that it doesn't even matter. The only reason it isn't the top spot on this list is because if someone is punching you in the butt, something strange has transpired. Why are they butt level with you while throwing punches? Why haven't you turned around to deal with them? Whatever the reality, you have probably found yourself in an unconventional kind of warfare, and I do wish you luck.

But like I said, there are some body locations where it's not ideal to be punched.

- **The stomach:** There's nothing cool about struggling to breathe when the air has been knocked out of you. This punch doesn't draw blood, but it does leave the person

---

5. Read that again. What I'm saying is that in the 1980s, Hollywood decided to make a movie where the central conflict revolved around a Sly Stallone character named Lincoln Hawk, who was arm-wrestling for money and the right to continued custody of his child. Also, the foe he had to conquer was named Bull Hurley. But what I'm also saying is that the potency of cocaine in the 1980s must have been really high.

who got punched acting as if they are trying to figure out breathing for the first time.

- **The face:** Here you've got maximum pain allocation while also having to wear the evidence of getting beat down as a kind of social shame.

- **The testicles:** This is the absolute worst place for a dude to get punched—it's not even up for debate. I know some guys claim that getting punched in the saddlebags is worse than giving birth, but that's dumb. Sure, it hurts very much, but compared to ejecting a human being out of your privates? *That* is a pain my gender will never, ever be able to understand.

Back to the fight. It took me a second to gather myself after the disorientation of being punched in the ear. But once I had, I heaved myself at Scott and managed to push him below his desk into the space where you slide your chair, and my goal was to cram him in there and trap him forever—or at the very least force him into a *127 Hours* situation in which, like James Franco, he would be faced with a decision between death or cutting off a limb to secure freedom. Unfortunately, Scott managed to escape, leaving each of us to lick our wounds in isolation.

For the seven days following this altercation, Scott slept in the Samford library; then, through our RA/mediator, we secured the transfer to different room assignments. I finished that semester and the next one with The Ferg, who introduced me to Jim Morrison, the Black Crowes, and Kate Hudson from the movie *Almost Famous*.[6] And Scott ended up with a repressed jock

---

6. The Ferg: the real MVP of my freshman year of college.

named Jason who eventually punched Scott so hard that he had to go to the hospital for stitches.

After our fistfight and extended avoidance of each other, I reconsidered my friendship with Scott and decided that, despite our history, it wasn't worth it anymore. It would be three more years before Scott and I spoke again.

If I can pay myself a weird compliment, I'm good at shedding unhealthy or unnecessary relationships. I know that this sounds like a psychotic quality, but I think when done healthily it is a huge advantage. Humans are inherently social beings, so we're always accumulating relationships—but are we ever reconsidering these relationships? Is that even something we feel we can do?

In a lot of ways we look at friendships like the email newsletters we subscribe to. I'm optimistic that subscribing to the Williams Sonoma newsletter might pay off with learning how to make the perfect grilled cheese. But usually I end up ignoring their emails and resenting their offers to help me master the art of the omelet. I don't even like omelets, Williams Sonoma—do you know anything about me? So I love that I intuitively know when to hit the Unsubscribe button on relationships and that I don't get bogged down feeling that I'm supposed to be all things to all people, and they to me. Sometimes it just isn't meant to be—and that's okay.

But just as this tendency toward unemotionality can be my blessing, it's a curse too. I cling to only my closest relationships as worth the time and energy of emotional maintenance, but then these few relationships have to bear the dense burden of expectation that most people spread out among many separate relationships.

This default tendency is something I've reconsidered in my head, but in all practicality I'm at a loss. In theory I know that the best friendships and relationships endure because you choose to continue that closeness, but in practice I can't help but harbor the idea that I might not be equipped to have numerous healthy relationships.

When I was younger I felt a certain pride about being a loner; it seemed to be my genetic birthright. So blowing up relationships or ghosting them wasn't a personality flaw. It was just "how God made me," so what could I do about this divine personality alchemy he'd mixed together?

But that's just an a-hole trying to justify his a-hole behavior. Sure, we're all predisposed to certain natures, but too often those predispositions become bastardized justifications for doing the easy things when the hard things are required.

Is it feasible to expect myself to become a social butterfly and interrelational dynamo? Not really. But that doesn't mean I can't try. Just because I can defer to my worse self doesn't mean I should.

More specifically, nothing is gained from being who you've always been. Reconsidering friendship and relationships and community has caused me to evolve both how I understand them and how I function within them.

You probably won't be surprised to hear that my relationship with Scott wasn't my only relationship falling-out that lasted for multiple years. I am fortunate that all of these falling-outs were able to be salvaged though. One relationship has turned into my best friend in the world, and Scott remains a very good friend to this day. He's such a good friend that I trust the insurance company he owns to cover my house and cars. The coverages are comprehensive, because you never know when life might sucker punch you right in the ear.

SEVEN

STREAKING AT A TACO BELL

Once, while I was in Omaha, Nebraska, with my best friends for the College World Series, we talked the most easily peer-pressured member of our group, Scott (yes, the same Scott from the previous chapter) into streaking through a Taco Bell drive-thru. But before I delineate the intricacies of this plan, both how it succeeded and how it failed, I should take a moment to outline the part of the Venn diagram where male friendships and the potentiality of streaking overlap.

While the act of streaking will be the main character of this chapter, the even-more-main character therein should be the vivid stupidity of young males, and how this vivid stupidity is a force that multiplies the more young males you gather together. Jesus said where three or more are gathered there is power,[1] and I believe this to be true. But additionally, where three or more twentysomething guys are gathered, there is a powerful possibility that something idiotic, illegal, or both is bound to happen.

---

1. Paraphrase of Matthew 18:20.

This is primarily because the older you get, the more the male decision-making dichotomy shifts. From birth until your midtwenties a lot of decisions are governed by a "Can I?" ideology.

Can I have that cookie?

Can I dodge that firework?

Can I convince that girl to like me?

Can I jump off that roof into that pool?

Let's collectively give thanks that, at a certain point, the balance shifts, and instead of rendezvousing[2] with the "Can I?" ideology, we begin to reconsider the wisdom of doing things just to see if we can do them. Because as we know, just because you *can* do something doesn't mean you should.

To this point, and specifically to this story, my friends Brennan, Andrew, and I lived to see if we could make Scott do dumb stuff. Not because we should have, but because we could.

And Scott, to his (dis)credit, was ever the repository for our goadings. But even more, Scott had a mystical ability to mis-play his hand so poorly that something even greater than the initial idea always ended up happening. So early on we realized that our ideas were often the appetizer leading into a better-but-unknowable main course.

The best example I can think of to illustrate this is when we goaded Scott into fighting a mutual friend during our free period in high school. The plan was for Scott to use the element of sur-prise and attack this friend with a soft-serve vanilla ice cream cone in the outdoor commons area so we could all watch.

When the time for the attack came, our friend blocked Scott's attempt and then reverse-smashed the ice cream cone directly

---

2. *Hamilton* reference.

into Scott's left nipple. This triggered Scott to scream in pain, which led to the friend shoving Scott away before continuing about his day. But the shoving sent Scott into the grassy area of the commons, where a sprinkler fired high-velocity water at his crotch from point-blank range. We could not have written a more hilariously satisfying scene. In many ways, what fueled us were the infinite possibilities of what could happen when Scott was at the helm of a bad idea.

But these things were always done in the comfort of our familiarities. We were finally ready to up the ante and see what we could convince Scott to do out in the real world.

The plan was to place our usual order (four cheesy gorditas), but instead of us driving around in our four-wheeled car, a naked Scott would walk around bipedally and approach the pick-up window, very casual and very au naturel. He would remit payment, collect our gorditas, and then jump back into the rental car with us to share a giant group LOL.[3]

When the time came to enact our plan, everything went off without a hitch. The gorditas were ordered, and Scott quickly unclothed himself for his approach to the drive-thru window. We exited the drive-thru lane and paralleled Scott's approach so we could behold the reaction, and the Taco Bell employees were about as enthused to behold Scott's nudity as you can imagine.

Scott grabbed the gorditas and prepared for his extraction, which is where things went awry.

See, we hadn't accounted for the possibility of police officers arriving on the scene in their car due to an obvious hungering

---

3. Important distinction if you are painting a mental image of this scene (and I do hope you are): Scott had shotgun so that when he dove back into the car, he could limit skin-to-genital contact and exposure.

for a Fourthmeal, but suddenly this hypothetical possibility was reality. The long arm of the Omaha law was now in full view of Scott sprinting naked toward our car.

For a second, time stood still. Brennan, Andrew, and I said nothing—except for whispered expletives. Scott froze like a deer in literal headlights, if a deer could also somehow be obscene. Reconsiderations abounded.

The policemen hit the brakes. Scott looked at them, then turned and looked back at us. It was like a scene from *The O.C.* when someone is about to get dramatically arrested and Imogen Heap's "Hide and Seek" is playing. Except none of us looked like anyone from *The O.C.*, this was Nebraska, and Scott was naked.

Suddenly the blue lights flipped on and the sirens blared. Scott immediately began crying. I'm not noting that detail to humiliate Scott. I think it adds a helpful texture to this moment in the story. It's all fun and games when your left nipple is assaulted with an ice cream cone outside the lunchroom, but being naked and afraid outside a Taco Bell hundreds of miles from home? That's a specific kind of vulnerability I don't ever want to know.

Both policemen erupted from their car, screaming at Scott to get dressed.

The rest of us didn't make a sound as Scott fetched his clothes from the front seat and nervously reclothed himself. We remained fervently silent in our haphazard parking spot while a policeman frisked Scott with the intensity of someone required to frisk John Wick.[4]

In fact, neither Brennan, Andrew, nor I made a single noise

---

4. I still don't know if the policemen were frisking Scott out of procedure or to mess with him. I mean, he had been previously naked and now he was wearing a Gap button-up with wrinkled khakis and boat shoes. He wasn't exactly *America's Most Wanted* material.

until we saw Scott get handcuffed. Partially because we didn't know how to deal with a friend who had been arrested but mostly because Scott's parents would know this was our fault because it most definitely *was* our fault.

Six days prior, before we left for Omaha, Scott's mother, Susan, had looked me squarely in the eyes and very distinctly said, "Take care of Scott." I'd laughed this off as though it were an exaggerated joke, but she repeated it gravely, not to be funny. She knew Scott's nature, and she knew our propensity for talking Scott into doing immensely stupid stuff.

Back in the present, even though I wasn't the one who'd just been naked, I couldn't shake off the feeling of shame.

After being handcuffed, Scott's crying intensified. Have you ever listened to a rainstorm turn into a thunderstorm and then into a hurricane-esque deluge of lightning, thunder, hail, and rain? That's what Scott's crying had evolved into. He cried so hard that it mutated into less a combination of tears and sniffles and more a combustion of snot, screams, and gagging noises. I'd never heard someone almost choke to death on their tears, but Scott was pretty much about to.

The effect of Scott's multisensory weeping experience on the police officers? They began to laugh at him, at first with their hands over their mouths in a stifled and respectable way. But this eventually gave way to full-on, bent-over, body-quaking laughter. One of them may have even pointed directly in Scott's face and laughed, though I can't be completely sure, as my memory does fail me from time to time.

The policemen were so physically exhausted from laughing that they were reborn into empathetic figures. They uncuffed Scott and let him off with a warning.

Scott silently returned to the car, and we silently accepted him. On the way back to the hotel, we wordlessly agreed to never have anything to do with streaking again. And then, saddest of all, we realized that Taco Bell hadn't given us gorditas; they'd given us chalupas. And they were cold.

I relate this story because it's fun, but also because there's a bigger takeaway that has stuck with me ever since: power and influence are real, and they come in wildly different and unexpected forms. This power might be as a parent or as the head of a team at work, or your work may influence people's beliefs and thoughts. Whatever situation you find yourself in, you have the power to influence people. So the question becomes, Are you going to wield that power to get someone to streak at a Taco Bell? Or are you going to wield it to help make the world a better place?

EIGHT

WAIT FOR IT[1]

SCENE:

My wedding day. I am in a hallway. Next to me stands my dad, and next to him stands a man, Keith, who is a kind of extended father-figure to me.

The hallway is white and spacious and quiet, but it's also hot. Like *so* hot. Like you can't even believe how hot this hallway is. It feels like a hallway on the surface of the sun. This hallway is so hot that if Sylvia Plath were still alive, she would try to stick her head somewhere inside.

Obviously, I'm sweating. Not just physically sweating, but emotionally too. Does that make sense? Have you ever emotionally sweated? If not, you should try it, except

---

1. Obvious *Hamilton* reference and my second-favorite *Hamilton* song.

I'm kidding. Don't do this. Emotional sweat
is like regular sweating but without the
catharsis of excretion.[2] Emotional sweat doesn't
register on your body, but it does register
in your overall vibe. Keith, who was also
the minister who would be facilitating the
marital ceremony, looked at me in a way
that suggested he could tell I was heavily
emotionally sweating.

KEITH

So, uh . . . everything okay?

ME

(like, not at all okay) Ha. Of course
I'm okay. Why? Do I not seem okay to
you? *(to no one and tugging at my
collar)* Is it me or does it feel like
the equator in here?

DAD

*(hands me a kerchief like a good best man
does)* You just look a little . . . pale?

ME

*(still not okay and also aware that I'm
suddenly very pale)* Do I?

---

2. I know, I'm not thrilled about having written that word either, but it's the only one I
could use to excrete the sentiment (do you see what I did there?).

CUT TO:

Me in the mirror looking like a
young Uncle Fester

DAD

(begins fanning me) Just breathe. Deep
breaths.

KEITH

And don't lock your knees.

ME

(suddenly panicked) What do you mean
don't lock my knees?

KEITH

If you lock your knees . . . *(makes
a falling whistle sound and, with his
hand, mimes me hitting the deck)*

Suddenly, I couldn't tell where the emotional sweat began and the physical sweat ended.

To be clear, I wasn't nervous and sweaty because I was unsure about my impending nuptials with Ashley.

Ashley and I were high school sweethearts. We'd endured heartache and distance and doubt, and we'd emerged victorious through the quagmire[3] of young love. In that moment, I was

---

3. *Hamilton* reference.

never surer of anything than I was of us, but therein was the problem. On the day we were married, I was twenty-one. Being sure about Ashley was the only thing in my life I really knew anything about.

Something I'm fascinated by is how we react to things we aren't prepared for. Emotionally, physically, spiritually, all that. There comes a time in everyone's lives when we're faced with something we have no idea how to handle. The first paycheck you receive, the first time you taste ice cream, and the first time you hear Elizabeth Holmes's voice—all are things you don't initially know how to process.

My mom told me that when I got stressed out as a kid, I would just lie down and fall asleep, as though my brain would survey the situation and be like, "Yeah, so, like, now is not a good time for me?"

In a way, I think that's what was happening on the day of my wedding. My mind was trying to process what was about to happen. The procedural part of the ceremony was no big deal. Ashley as my lifetime partner? Perfect, and everything I'd always wanted. But the deeper, more existential aspect of what all this meant was conjuring up all kinds of fear and worry. I wasn't just changing my profile status from single to married. I now was a spouse—and even more, I also had a spouse whom I had to put before myself, and not just in a let-her-pick-the-movie-some-nights way. In an in-sickness-and-in-health way. In an I-love-this-person-more-than-myself way.

When I was younger, it had been hard enough dealing with

my own weirdo complexities. What would it mean to have to be there for someone else too?

This worry extended into wondering not only if I could be enough for her but also if I could be so much "enough" that I could make her happy. I hadn't thought about this in such immediate terms. No one had told me that "enough" and "happy" were totally different things, and here I was about to be married. No one had spoken a word about the expansive void of nothingness between the marital feelings of "enough" and "happy."

What if, as a spouse and partner, my best effort exists in the wasteland between "enough" and "happy"?

A lot of this ignorance and urgency was because of my age. I was twenty-one—and not a savvy, grizzled twenty-one. A soft twenty-one. In terms of mental and emotional toughness, I was softer than puppy turds.

I was intellectually soft too. There were still moments in life where, when faced with something difficult, my impulse was to search for an adult to help me.

BANKER

Are you familiar with amortization?

ME

(looks around for an adult) I definitely am, like so much. But why don't you explain it to me, just so we can both be sure that we're talking about the same thing?

MECHANIC

Do you know what happens when you don't rotate your tires?

ME

They get tired out?

MECHANIC

(stare of death)

ME

It was a joke. Did you get it? Should I do it again?

MECHANIC

Seriously, do you know what happens when you don't rotate your tires?

ME

(whispers in the smallest voice possible)
They get tired out?

MECHANIC

(stares at me)

ME

(looks around for an adult)

DOCTOR'S OFFICE RECEPTIONIST

Have you met your deductible yet?

ME

No, is he here?

DOCTOR'S OFFICE RECEPTIONIST

What?

ME

My bad, is she here?

DOCTOR'S OFFICE RECEPTIONIST

You do know what a deductible is,
right?

ME

(looks around for an adult)

On a deeper level all this anxiety was related to a hyper-awareness of feeling like a fraud. Feeling that I was a little kid acting like an adult, and that I was about to make Ashley join me in an extended charade where we formed one composite adult by one of us standing on the other's shoulders under a trench coat.

That was the panic: that my incompetence at life wasn't just my cross to bear anymore; it was hers too.

One of my best friends in the world, Andrew, got married in 2018. Ashley and I attended the wedding, and it was the first wedding I'd been to in several years. As such, it was the first one where I could finally recognize and appreciate the occasion for what it was.

It's like rewatching a really good movie with someone who has never seen it. You know where the narrative arcs and character development are leading, so you are doubly invested, both in picking up small aspects you missed the first time around and in getting to observe the other person's experience.

At my wedding I missed so much because I was so nervous and preoccupied with things like my own emotional imposter syndrome and not locking my knees, but watching Andrew, I was reminded about all the things I'd glossed over: the ancientness of the ceremony, the audacious sanctity of what the vows meant, the beautiful community of people gathered in support. It was enough to make me a little misty-eyed.

Andrew and I are the same age, and at the time of his marriage, Ashley and I were about to celebrate our fourteenth anniversary. At our wedding we were tiny little baby children. Our ceremony may as well have consisted of juice boxes, Lunchables, and nap time. So Andrew's experience and my experience with marriage were already different.

I'd always admired Andrew for his self-assuredness of what he wanted in life. I remember he took a gap year in college and worked in St. Thomas just for the life experience. I couldn't wrap my head around such an idea. First, because all I wanted to do was get beyond college, so the idea of extending it seemed insane. Second, it seemed such a daredevil move. To just go away? And live somewhere else? Can you even do that? What if you need an adult?

In retrospect, it was brilliant, because Andrew was aware of something then that I'm only now realizing: you have to take advantage of moments and seasons so that you can better understand who you are and who you want to be. Right now, in my midthirties, I'm just kick-starting that process. How much better of a husband could I have been if I'd not been so young and dumb?

There have been many times that I wished Ashley and I had been older when we got married. Ashley had never lived on her own, and I barely had by only the most generous application of the idea. We will encourage our kids to consider marriage later in life, only after they've established the bedrock of who they want to be professionally and emotionally. This is because, in my experience, the person you are at twenty is very different from the person you are at thirty-six. There's no perfect age for marriage, but there's a good balance to be struck in letting life and experience marinate you while your metabolism is still on your side.

But as much as I would have loved to be more competent and qualified as a spouse, after reconsidering where Ashley and I are now versus where we started,[4] I would do it again the exact same way. Yes, we were breathtakingly stupid. Yes, we were astonishingly naïve, and yes, we were unbelievably selfish, but we were stupid, naïve, and selfish together.

---

4. *Hamilton* reference.

The identities we have now were forged separately, but also kind of separately together. Does that make sense? I swear I'm not trying to be confusing in an attempt to be cute; "separately together" makes a ton of sense to me, both as an introvert and as one-half of a relationship that had a lot of growing up to do.

Ashley and I are both exceedingly different from who we were at twenty and twenty-one, respectively, but we became different *together*. And that has created a love and closeness that can't be explained. Our relationship isn't perfect, but it is ours. We laugh, and we cry, and we break, and we make our mistakes,[5] but we do it all together. When that happens, you develop a certain collaborative armor. Getting married as young as we did isn't for the faint of heart, and I probably wouldn't recommend it, but I'm so very, very glad we did it.

---

5. *Hamilton* reference.

NINE

SEX SCENES

Look, I'm not here to be your dad, and I'm the last person anyone would accuse of being puritanical. But the reason I'm asking for this reconsideration is because of a larger mystery: For whom exactly are we still doing sex scenes in television and film? (I mean, besides Harvey Weinstein.[1]) In a lot of ways sex scenes feel like a bizarre anachronism, like the human appendix or the Rolling Stones; sure, I get *why* they are here, but why are they *still* here?

So let's break this down. Foundationally we have to acknowledge the roguish element motivating scenes of sexy time. Caveman art might be the purest form of art because it was done without the larger pursuit of cultural fame, but it included renditions of sex because even cavemen loved the visuality of the forbidden.

Fast-forward a great many years and that idea of visualizing the forbidden endures. After the invention of the cinema,

---

1. That was a solid #MeToo burn, you guys. It may have been more topical in 2018, but just assume that in the moment it was typed, this was a savagery.

sex scenes weren't far behind, because their inclusion allowed a wink/nudge way of contextualizing nudity for the sake of appropriately consuming it. A bare boob or butt is just a bare boob or butt, but in service to a story line? Now that boob or butt contains multitudes. In the same way that comedy exists as the subversion of expectation, thus our reaction to laugh, so, too, can nudity and sex on film exist to provoke the audience toward a deeper understanding of a character or the relationship between characters.

And to play devil's advocate for a moment, I can understand this. There's a filmmaking maxim about showing the audience something instead of telling them about it, and sex scenes certainly fulfill the former idea in a more memorable way. But modern sex scenes seem less like character/plot development and more like cultural catnip, and this line of demarcation separating pornography and art seems to be about as thin as the different priorities in making them. It's the difference between porn and *Basic Instinct*. And if you try to serve both, congratulations: you've just made *Showgirls*, starring Elizabeth Berkley.

We know that sex sells, and something that leans in the direction of sex will always get our attention. This base fascination with sex is probably the pervy underbelly of its persistence, so I realize that sex scenes in art will probably be intertwined with our species for as long as we endure.

But the weird thing is that you rarely hear the existence of sex scenes litigated. Sex scenes just *are*. There's this sense that they've always been and they always will be. There certainly are conversations about the validity, appropriateness, and sometimes necessity of sex scenes, but that's as evaluative as we get.

People get more granular about movies or television shows using voice-over or breaking the fourth wall than they do about sex scenes and nudity. Which I get, because who in the whole self-respecting world wants to be the tip of the spear on academically breaking down sex scenes like they're the Zapruder film? Because we don't deeply consider sex scenes and nudity out of not wanting to appear gauche, there is no check and balance, no reconsideration of their actual function. Isn't that the reason they continue to exist?

Think about it: we've managed to mostly annihilate laugh tracks, and once Adam Sandler retires, we'll be super close to killing the trope of a gross, weirdo slob-man being able to marry a Victoria's Secret model. But for some reason, the potential reconsideration of why sex scenes persist on TV and in movies has yet to even be proposed.

Speaking of Adam Sandler, really quickly here are my ten most favorite hot girl / not guy pairings that TV or movies have inexplicably asked us to accept as believable.

1. Jessica and Roger Rabbit
2. Jerry Seinfeld and every love interest on *Seinfeld* ever[2]
3. Kevin James and Leah Remini on *The King of Queens*
4. Cece and Schmidt on *New Girl*
5. Andy and Ann from *Parks and Recreation*
6. Adam Sandler and Brooklyn Decker in *Just Go with It*
7. Jay and Gloria from *Modern Family*
8. Everyone opposite Austin Powers
9. WALL-E and EVE
10. Milo and Otis

---

2. Specifically, I'll never forgive Jerry Seinfeld and Larry David for coming up with an episode premise in which we are supposed to believe that Jerry Seinfeld, a person who looks like the assistant manager at a furniture store, would be ambivalent about Teri Hatcher. It makes me so mad I almost cannot breathe.

Again, though, I want to be clear. My motivation behind pressing for a reassessment of sex scenes isn't because of my delicate sensibilities or because I'm a closeted Puritan. It's more because I don't think any of us can identify the moment where, collectively, we were all like, "Yes, let's definitely keep installing sex scenes in our mass media." Even a more thoughtful contemplation about these scenes would mitigate some of the bad habits that have developed around their utility.

For example, nudity and sexual situations are like curse words in your vocabulary. They definitely communicate something, but too much of them only communicates all the wrong things.

Also, you can communicate intimacy without showing naked bodies slapping together. One of my favorite shows, *Better Call Saul*, has never shown the lead couple having sex despite clearly being in a romantic relationship. This is partially because no one wants to see Bob Odenkirk in flagrante delicto, but it's mostly because the show's writers do the work of showing the two characters doing things like wordlessly sharing a cigarette in a dark alley. It's not very titillating,[3] but it accomplishes what the writers are angling for.

But probably most importantly, nothing on God's heavenly green earth can be worth the awkwardness of watching an unexpected sex scene with people you weren't mentally prepared to watch a sex scene with. I'll never ever forget watching *Munich* with my mom and dad and suffering through the scene where Eric Bana has cathartic sex with his wife. No one should ever be subjected to cathartic-Eric-Bana-sex while sitting in close

---

3. How do we feel about this word even existing? Is it ever used where everyone unanimously responds like, "Perfect usage and we all feel great about it"?

proximity to their parents. I'm not trying to yuck anyone's yum, but that arrangement just isn't right.

There's no call to action here and I'm not writing this to persuade you to march on Hollywood or boycott anything tangentially connected to sexualized scenes. This is more observational in a sort of (extreme Jerry Seinfeld voice) "What's the deal with sex scenes?" kind of way, because it seems strange that we're weirdly accepting of the reality that during our consumption of some pop culture, we may be surprised by abrupt, superfluous nudity and/or genital close-ups. Whether that is or is not your thing, I'm not here to judge, but I think it's worth reconsidering the institution of stylized nudity and unrealistic sex.

TEN

MASCULINITY

In 2018 the Gillette razor company released a television advertisement called "We Believe: The Best Men Can Be" that sought to intertwine the market's need for razors with our culture's need for reformed masculinity. If you aren't familiar with this commercial or don't remember it well, I urge you to look it up on YouTube, because it wasn't really about razors at all.

The ad took dead aim at masculinity in an unprecedented but also transfixing way. We get a montage juxtaposing different iterations of problematic behavior, some overt and obnoxious and others more subtle and casually systemic, all in pursuit of an idea that men can do better by holding themselves and others accountable. It is astoundingly precise in its commentary on the conflict between new wave and traditional masculinity, and the idea that this was precipitated by Gillette is truly wild.

For a while before the Gillette ad, brands had been reluctant to deeply dip their toes in the waters of social and cultural awareness. But the Gillette ad was jolting because of how directly it sought to address such a critical cultural issue.

Broadly speaking, nothing will incur cynicism more readily than a brand advocating for a certain moral or social position. And this Gillette ad came on the heels of another campaign with a similar social consciousness: Nike's full support of Colin Kaepernick just prior to the 2018 Super Bowl. Kaepernick's status as a symbol of cultural importance stemmed from his silent protest of racism and police brutality by kneeling during the national anthem while he was a quarterback for the San Francisco 49ers in 2016. Colin Kaepernick's protest is an entirely different issue reserved for an entirely different conversation; however, both Nike and Gillette chose to make statements that were guaranteed to be misconstrued by certain segments of the population (and almost willfully misconstrued by specific segments).

Wherever you stand on the nobility or cynicism of those public statements, we cannot disentangle the corporate interest informing them. These companies obviously anticipated the notoriety and conversation their statements would generate for their brands. We'll never know for sure how much of a factor self-promotion versus moral urgency was in the decision to pursue these tracks. Because we cannot identify the motivation of the ad, we cannot truly evaluate it.

But we can evaluate the *existence* of this ad and what that existence suggests about not just the evolution of advertising but the cultural climate and conversations therein. Corporate entities speaking on societal trends feels strange and weird because it is strange and weird. The blurring of lines that occurs when a company I sometimes buy razors from also attempts to educate me on how to be a man and how to raise my son is beyond bizarre. But it isn't without merit.

One of my favorite genres is true crime. I like procedurals and I like zombie movies, but I really love true crime because the stories are connected to something real and true. In many cases, even if tragedy occurs, there is ultimately some reckoning for the antagonists.

Specifically, within my professional sphere, true-crime podcasts shows are a juggernaut. Broadly speaking, they all share a similar rhythm: there is a crime that has gone unpunished, and the host(s) of the podcast spend seven to ten episodes attempting to solve the crime as a way to bring closure to the victim(s). Sometimes they do, sometimes they don't, and sometimes their detective work tips over enough dominos that new evidence emerges. But in most cases, the successful shows take a story with a dead end and improve upon it in some way.

It's a saturated category not only because most people like the genre but also because there's a ton of content to be mined. If podcasting is California in the mid-1800s, then true-crime podcasters are the panhandlers who keep finding gold, because there are a lot of unsolved cases out there.

To say that the true-crime podcast boom is a result of the failure of law enforcement is roundly unfair. Law enforcement is handcuffed (nailed it) in terms of the time, tools, and attention it is allowed to dedicate to a single crime. But there is a correlation between their resources and the amount of unsolved cases available to enterprising amateur detectives. When these shows are produced, they represent a fascination with story, yes, but they mostly represent a market inefficiency. In other words, the multitude of unsolved mysteries, crimes, and murders has given rise to a third estate of sorts to help deal with a demand that has wildly outpaced the supply of people who can contend with it.

This is similar to a "Paving for Pizza" promotion I saw Domino's Pizza highlight recently. The goal is for Domino's to subsidize the paving of roads throughout all fifty states. The purpose is clear: potholes and broken roads compromise the ability of Domino's to quickly and cleanly deliver delicious pizza. But the subtext is that our local governments are failing on such a prolific level that a company from the private sector has to step in to protect their interests so that their business isn't affected. Again, the favor Domino's is trying to curry isn't without its own selfish interest attached, but there is enough of a market inefficiency that it muddies the water on how much Domino's is being noble versus being *shrewdly* noble.

Which brings us back to Gillette. Wherever you land on the commercial, Gillette is stepping into the masculinity conversation because, culturally, there is a market inefficiency in communicating what masculinity is versus what it should be. And we should see this as a profound, systemic failure.

As a practicing Christian, I feel like this failure is a blaring indictment of evangelical Christianity, which has long been too content to sit out of conversations that pertain to race, sexuality, and gender equality. I can't decide if this is a conscious decision as much as it is a generalized masculine inability to articulate little else than what we do not support.[1]

I don't want to appear as if I'm simplifying a nuanced conversation about a difficult idea that most inhabitants of said toxic masculinity aren't even conscious of. Similarly nuanced

---

1. See John MacArthur, re: Beth Moore, diversity, etc.

is the generational friction of the elder generations, who are resentful that they have to evolve, adapt, and pay attention to the sensibilities of others, and the younger generations, who are hypersensitive and almost hysterically reactive.

Physicality and power are inextricably linked to masculinity, as is a kind of privilege—all of which complicate an already complex topic. Are we talking about what makes someone masculine? Are we talking about the baggage that comes with toxic masculinity? Are we allowing for the idea that masculinity is redeemable, or are we just presuming it to be something inherently awful and broken?

There's a contingent who think that masculinity is under siege, and they aren't entirely wrong. It is, but that siege is a direct result of masculinity's own inability to articulate and govern itself. This inarticulate, historically unregulated version of masculinity is feeling the heat because it draws its power from being in a position of privilege, but now that reality is shifting. Women need men less than they used to—both as breadwinners and as the other variable in a procreation scenario. But this evolution isn't a threat to topple masculinity altogether, just the iteration that relies on the imbalance of power and opportunity.

As a man myself and as the father of a son, I'm daily reconsidering what it means to be a man. As much as I wish that I had a clarified definition, I don't. But I do think that the first step to gaining that clarification in a tumultuous world is to have that conversation. To reconsider. To prosecute the elements that should be criticized and celebrate the aspects that should be celebrated.

And as much as I don't love a razor company educating me on what it means to be a man, I appreciate them trying to kick-start that conversation, even if they're trying to sell me on a close shave at the same time.

PART TWO

RECONSIDER LIFE

Listen to your life. See it for the fathomless mystery
it is. In the boredom and pain of it, no less than
in the excitement and gladness: touch, taste, smell
your way to the holy and hidden heart of it, because
in the last analysis all moments are key moments,
and life itself is grace.

—FREDERICK BUECHNER

ELEVEN

PARTICIPATION TROPHIES

Participation trophies have gotten a bad rap. They are both the manifestation of millennial incompetence and the symbolic undoing of our once great nation—the idea being that even more than drugs, pornography, or food delivery services, participation trophies are the real reason that America is not what she once was. This is a fanatical absurdity if you scrutinize the notion even a little. But it's hard to offer that scrutiny, because the connective tissue between participation trophies and the wussification and entitlement of young Americans is so strong. The connection appears almost impossible to reconsider, such is its cosmic truthfulness.

But it's not really true at all, cosmically or otherwise.

At some point the conversation about the worth of providing recognition to elementary school–aged children was co-opted into a larger commentary about generational differences. This is not abnormal. Older generations have always relentlessly resented subsequent generations because of the increased easiness with which they endure life. For example, a few years after I graduated high school, the school's football games were broadcast on TV and the administration signed an athletic apparel deal with Nike, leading to stylish uniforms and free Nike swag. To this day, I hate those younger classes with a fiery passion because they have no idea how lucky they are. I had to buy my own Nike products at the sporting goods store, like an animal.

And that's just how it goes: the Olds always think that the Younglings are just soft little candy babies who don't really understand what it took to settle the frontier or walk the 362 miles to school in twenty-eight feet of snow. But for some reason (and I don't know if this is unique to our modern setup or if every generation finds a physical manifestation of this frustration) the participation trophy has become symbolic of this generational divide. Not because it is apt, mind you, but because it is convenient.

The first problem we detect upon reconsidering participation trophies is that participation trophies aren't even a modern innovation. In fact, according to a piece written by Stefan Fatsis for *Slate*,[1] they emerged onto the scene just after World War I.[2] From there the concept migrated to college campuses to motivate students to exercise and work hard, then eventually made its way onto military bases both before and after World War II. So to pretend that millennials demanded participation trophies into

1. Stefan Fatsis, "We've Been Handing Out Participation Trophies for 100 Years," *Slate*, April 10, 2019, https://slate.com/culture/2019/04/participation-trophy-history-world -war-i.html.
2. Read that again. If you are scoring at home, that makes the participation trophy decidedly not a millennial innovation. And even more, there's a bigger conversation to be had about this specific subset of decision makers, because along with initiating the scourge of participation trophies, they also enacted Prohibition, which was a uniformly terrible idea with unintended consequences of proliferating organized crime and drug cartels. But yeah, millennials and their avocado toast, am I right?

existence to further fuel a generational appetite for empty praise and entitlement is just aggressively incorrect.

Moreover, doing so ignores the fact that the very existence of participation trophies is a tradition approved and passed along by every generation since the Silent Generation.[3] This is an important distinction because the stereotypical articulation of participation trophies also overlooks the idea that Baby Boomers and Gen Xers perpetuated this tradition.

The entire mechanism of participation trophies is greased and operated by older generations, who then weirdly use it to indict the very generation they subconsciously feel compelled to reward. It's ridiculous. I'm trying to talk about this in a logical way, but it is a magnificently idiotic absurdity. It would be like me inventing Nutella, manufacturing it, giving it to my children, making them eat it, and then weaponizing their subsequent affection for Nutella as an indicator of something I don't like about their generation.

Let's attempt some amateur pop psychology to understand this haphazard handling of participation trophies by older generations. Could it be that they are caught within the tension of both sensing the tradition has flaws (the empty meaning of participation and how rewarding it could create a feeling of entitlement) and being motivated by increasingly modern anxieties to be more emotionally present and protective of their children? Has this led to their begrudging acceptance and encouragement of participation trophies even though they see the trend as an ultimate net negative?

It's even more important to think of participation trophies from the receiving generation's perspective. After all, there is no

---

3. Those born in 1945 and before. I don't have anything snarky to say; I'm just trying to be helpful.

youth league union composed of kids demanding a trophy or ribbon for their time and energy spent playing T-ball. And as a millennial with kids who are also participating in athletic leagues, I can confidently say that most of us value these trophies exactly not at all. They are less an accomplishment or brick in the foundations of our worldviews and more a cheap physical punctuation on our athletic experiences. Suggesting that they exist as something more profound to anyone involved is projecting wildly.

To wrap up and put a bow on this idea of participation trophies, if you reconsider the general idea behind them—regardless of what generation you belong to—are they really that bad? In my experience there is never any uncertainty about where kids fall in the social and athletic strata of a community, and a participation trophy does nothing to confuse this. Instead, offering participation trophies provides an opportunity for inclusivity, something that quickly dissolves for most kids, if it ever existed in the first place, especially within athletics.

And if you are frustrated with the idea of a child feeling a moment of unanimous inclusion because you think that this somehow represents a larger referendum on the failures of society, I can promise you that the failure isn't with society; it's with you.

TWELVE

BIRTHDAYS

Birthdays are stupid and pointless. Hear me out.

Everything about a birthday is arbitrary. You have no choice in when yours is, and you have no recourse in changing it. Most everything else in life you can change: your name, your eye color, where you live, even your face (expensively via plastic surgery or economically via Snapchat). But not your birthday. Your date of birth is stamped upon your identity as this definitive thing, even though the meaning and definition of how your birthday manifests in your life shape-shifts fairly regularly.

When you're young, your birthday is a seminal event, and it is used as a marker for not just you but also your parents to denote your acceleration through life. This is why parents hilariously age their kids by months early in the game. Small children will humble you so much that every month you keep them alive and your sanity intact feels like something to be celebrated. Parents are aware that presenting their son Jaxton to you as "forty-eight months old" is patently absurd, but "four years" doesn't represent all the blood, sweat, and tears that have gone into Jaxton's preservance. Olympics and presidential elections happen once every four years, but Jaxton tests their sanity to live every single minute of every day.

Have you considered how malleable the birthday celebration is? Consider the following important year markers and what they exist to celebrate:

- **Age one:** Your parents kept you alive for an entire calendar year.
- **Age three:** Your parents can begin signing you up for all the activities as a subconscious attempt to fill the hole in their hearts about failing at baseball/gymnastics/soccer/ dance/football/basketball.
- **Age ten:** You are a decade old, which makes every parent intensely feel the passage of time, and for a brief moment they consider having another kid.
- **Ages eleven through eighteen:** One of your birthdays in this range is probably going to be ruined by proximity to a sex talk.
- **Age thirteen:** You begin developing terrible taste in art and music, commemorated by the gifts you request of others.[1]
- **Age sixteen:** This birthday is a zero-sum game in pursuit of a car.
- **Age eighteen:** You can be apathetic about voting and enthusiastic about opening a credit card account, which you will immediately abuse.
- **Age twenty-one:** This birthday is important only for drinking reasons.

---

1. In 2001, I unironically asked for the CD *Weathered*, by Creed.

After this, the only other birthday of note is when you get old enough to qualify for senior-citizen discounts.

So my question is this: After the age of twenty-one, why do we continue observing this mostly ceremonial holiday? Because the birthdays definitely don't get better.

In fact, they are very much like our reactions to Alec Baldwin. Early birthdays are like Alec in *Glengarry Glen Ross*. We were like, "Great! Love this Baldwin guy! He's so masculine and metropolitan." Adolescent/teenage/twenties birthdays are like when we all realized Alec had so many brothers: "Oh cool! He has brothers; maybe they will be great too!" And post-thirty birthdays are like Alec doing the Trump impression on *Saturday Night Live*: "Is there any way for someone to help me feed myself to a shark?"[2]

The obvious answer for why we continue celebrating birthdays is that they are entrenched identifiers, and entrenched stuff is so difficult to undo. Look at daylight savings. We all agree it is ridiculous and dumb and a huge hassle. First, you have to remember springing forward and falling back and whatever those things mean. Do you spring forward on the clock because you are so well rested from that extra hour of sleep? But daylight savings time persists because figuring out how to harmonize everyone in the cessation of observance feels more overwhelming than just losing all sense of time and place two weekends a year.

But truly, birthdays remain because the entire notion of your date of birth is profoundly self-centered. A birthday commemorates the day you traded in the comfort of a womb for the variable

---

2. One time, I was at a Starbucks and a barista told me I looked like a Baldwin brother. I pressed her for which Baldwin brother specifically, and she refused to cite an exact one, leading me to believe that she meant Daniel Baldwin.

insanity of this nonwomb world. And that's a big deal! What an important event. Except, what if your actual birthdate sucks?

My birthday is 12/21, which sounds not too terrible, right? It's a palindrome, which is cool. Also, it's kind of close to Christmas, which is probably great—except, wait, sorry, actually, it is completely *not*.

You know how there's a death zone for climbers ascending Everest, where the human body just cannot exist for an extended amount of time? That's the same for birthdays within a five-day radius of Christmas. Authentic celebration or appreciation just can't happen on an individual level because Jesus and Santa gobble up all the shine.

You might be thinking, *But, Knox, you're not a child anymore. Surely you aren't complaining about not getting more gifts on your birthday.*

And to that I say, it's not about the gifts. I don't even *like* gifts. The best gift for an introvert is the time and space to guiltlessly conduct their own solitude. And now that I'm older, I'm convinced this is true for most people, whether they're introverts or not. I don't want a party or a big to-do or even a piñata.[3] I just want some time and space to do what I want to celebrate the day of my birth. And even more, I want a day that isn't overshadowed by Jesus' birthday. There, I said it. No shade to Jesus, but his birthday tends to suck up all the oxygen in the room for the entire month. Is it too much to ask to not have to share time with white elephant parties, Dirty Santa parties, passive-aggressive relatives reluctantly visiting with their toddlers and exposing everyone to H1N1, and also the birth of the Savior?

---

3. This is an abject lie. Everyone wants a piñata always. No exceptions.

But this is my lot in life, and I guess I just have to bear this birthday burden. Unless . . .

What if we reconsider birthdays?

What if, after the age of twenty-one, you get a birthday rumspringa? What if you could experiment with moving your birthday to a different season altogether to see how it feels? And if you like it, you keep it, and it is reflected in your permanent records.

For some of you, no change is needed. And that's great for you. I'm so happy that you have a perfectly placed, between-holidays birthday with no natural rivals for everyone's attention. Truly, great job, you.

But others of us want to exercise some agency in when the world is asked to celebrate us. I'm not thinking solely of myself here either—there are people out there with the following birthdates:

- **January 1:** There are so many things to start the year with that are immeasurably more exciting than celebrating your birthday: college football, working out, picking out a new journal/planner that you will stop using in 4.5 days.
- **February 14:** Through no fault of your own, you are cursed to share calendar space with the commercialization of love. Thoughts and prayers to you.
- **February 29:** I honestly have no idea how birthdays work in the leap year realm. Do they count? Are they doubled? Tripled? Is this how Paul Rudd is technically fifty but obviously not really fifty? I'm not being hyperbolic: the leap year is truly like the Bermuda Triangle of the calendar, and I cannot be expected to understand such mysteries.

- **April 1:** Whenever you get sad, think for a second about all that these people have had to endure because their birthday falls on April Fools' Day.
- **July 4:** As dysfunctional as America gets, you're never going to be able to compete with hot dogs, fireworks, pool parties, and independence.
- **October 31:** I'm not the kind to make cheap trick-or-treat jokes, but if I were, one would go here.
- **November 14:** Congrats! You get to celebrate your birthday knowing that your parents had sex on Valentine's Day!
- **December 20-31:** Reason-for-the-season (that is specifically not you) excitement and then post–reason-for-the-season fatigue. Also, on New Year's Eve, no one knows what to do, but the one thing they do know is that it shouldn't be attending a birthday party for you.

If you are the holder of any of these birthdates, imagine the freedom of being able to literally change the calendar for yourself.

I've got my eyes set on a June 20 birthday. It's two weeks after my dad's birthday and two weeks before the Fourth of July, and it allows me to celebrate by doing what I love most: hanging out poolside, grilling delicious meats, and not having to contort my schedule around a holiday or school calendar. So I call dibs on that one. But for every other day, I invite you to reconsider what it means to grow a year older.

THIRTEEN

THE HALF-MARATHON MAN

I'm on a bus. Not a school bus, and certainly not a magical one. It's the public transit type, and it's for transit in Nashville, specifically for the Country Music Marathon. It's April 2008, and I'm running the half marathon as a nonrunning runner. Does that sound confusing or counterintuitive? Let me explain.

I don't run for the high of running; I run to quell the guilt I have over things like gorging myself on pounds of pulled pork and drizzling the butterful bejeezus out of my extra-large popcorn every time I go see a movie. Still, that doesn't explain why I would escalate things to the point where I'm getting ready to run a half marathon and also working through an entry-level panic attack.

The real explanation for being on that bus was that our first child was due later that year, and I could correctly assess two things about myself: I was monstrously selfish, and I rarely challenged myself to do hard things.

People like to romanticize the moment a child is born as a seminal moment, which it totally is. I know that the previous sentence reads like I was going to zig where most people zag, but I'm not. Babies getting born is dope, full stop. But we don't spend enough time deep-diving into the mental situation of expectant parents when they realize that a birth is seven-to-eightish months imminent.

That's a different mental state because, though the information you are receiving is transcendent, there's no immediate experience that follows to release the pressure of anticipation. You just have to sit in the existential space of knowing that your life is about to change—but not anytime soon. In this space many parents are hit with the reality that they themselves need to change.

I knew that my son's arrival would demand a shift in the typical orbit of my worldview. Pre–Ashley being pregnant, I was selfish in the way that all childless people are. To be clear, I don't mean to do a drive-by generalizing all childless people as selfish in a pejorative sense. But a child forces you to consider them first in all things, and the repetition of this exercise over time—of always considering someone else first—makes people with children more predisposed to unselfish behavior. This obviously isn't to say that childless people can't be unselfish; it's just something they have to seek out more actively than, say, a parent who has to juggle playdate specifics, dietary restrictions, bedtime routines, and emotional development.

I knew I had to reconsider my understanding of the world almost immediately because I knew that as soon as our son emerged into this world, everything was going to get more difficult—not in a bad way, but in a "more is about to be required of us" way. But I didn't know specifically what that would mean, and I didn't know how I would handle this unspecified difficulty because of all the unspecificity.

So I decided to take matters into my own hands by trying to simulate different difficult things in advance of my son's birth. Which is why running a half marathon kind of made sense.[1] This plan felt progressive and wise, and I secretly took a lot of self-satisfied intellectual triumph laps congratulating myself at being so forward-thinking.

However, the self-congratulating came to a halt when I had to start training for the half marathon. For clarification, I wasn't a stranger to running. I'd been a casual runner since college, but not in the way I would need to run to be fully prepped for the race. That prep involved miles of consistent running every week—and not a meager portion of miles either. In the latter portion of my training, I was going to have to put in significant mileage so that I would be ready for the entire 13.1-mile course.

My signing up for the marathon also came with a set of shoulder angels. Good Knox Shoulder Angel[2] would encourage me to run and remind me of why I was training. But Bad Knox Shoulder Angel[3] liked to point out how difficult running was, how long it was taking me, and how my son would never appreciate the symbolic significance of this experience. And I must say, Bad Knox Shoulder Angel was much more succinct and persuasive[4] with his arguments than Good Knox Shoulder Angel.

---

1. In retrospect, this makes less than zero sense, FYI. It was a choice, sure. Not a great choice, but what I'm arguing here is that you have to respect the specificity of the choice. (You absolutely do *not* have to do that, but whatever, Book Knox.)
2. Think of me in all white, clean-shaven, chubby(ier) cheeked, and downright cherubic in almost every way.
3. Now think of me in black-and-red leather, with weirdly and specifically designed facial hair and wearing sunglasses indoors. Also, let's toss in a puka shell necklace for good measure, because I would love to be able to pull that off, and this seems the perfect occasion to attempt something like that.
4. *Hamilton* reference.

Accordingly, my resolve wore down over time. Partially because the adrenaline of the original excitement and commitment was wearing off and partially because running in general kind of sucks.

After maxing out at five-mile training runs, I decided to bail. I was out the registration money and the cash I paid for my custom-fit Nike running shoes (super LOL), but I promised myself that I would prepare for fatherhood in other, less physically exhausting ways.

A few weeks after making that decision, Ashley and I were at a birthday party for a family friend. It was a week before the marathon, and I hadn't exactly gone public with my lack of intention to run. In fact, only Ashley knew that I wasn't planning to go forward. But when we saw my parents at the party, my mom inquired about my training.

MOM

So are you ready for the half marathon?

KNOX

(sheepishly) I actually don't think I'm going to do it.

MOM

How come?

KNOX

(a buffet of tepid excuses)

MOM

Yeah, well, I was going to be surprised
if you ended up running it.

Those words stung me hard.

My mom wasn't being hurtful, and she definitely wasn't wrong. Running a half marathon *was* entirely out of character for me. But that was the exact reason I originally felt I needed to do it. And if the occasion of becoming a father wasn't significant enough for me to change my ways, what did that say about my character? Sure, the correlation between my running and my being a good dad was still not really simpatico with any kind of logic, but it was very much harmonized in a metaphorical sense; if I was going to flake so easily on this, what else might I be compelled to flake on?

This deep reconsideration led me to realize that I had to run that half marathon, and I had only a week to get ready.

One week later, I'm in Nashville sitting on that bus, emotionally hyperventilating and nervously sweating through two layers of Under Armour clothing.

The bus is full of people headed to the starting line of the half marathon. I don't know where I'm supposed to go. I don't know if I have the proper paperwork to run. I don't know if I've inadvertently entered a race loaded with Super Kenyans who are going to leave me in the dust. My biggest nightmare—beyond my heart spontaneously exploding because I never even got close to training for the full distance of the race—is that I might finish dead last. The night before, I had nightmares about it: Dream Me is moving at such a slow pace that the organizers are actively closing down the course behind me so that normal traffic patterns can resume in the wake of my pathetic slowfullness.

The bus is so loud. Everyone around me seems excited to take on the challenge they've spent months preparing for, but I'm overwhelmed with stress and guilt and fear. My pregnant wife is still asleep back at a disgusting motel, which was the best we could do because I'd waited until literal days before the race to book a room. It's the kind of motel where you open a drawer and a roach skitters out and around to evade detection. If this is a metaphor for how I'm going to be as a father, I'm off to a terrible start, while also managing to shoehorn in some failure as a husband.

To calm myself, I try to focus on three goals: (1) don't die, (2) don't finish last, and (3) don't walk. These are my mantras. They are simple, they are doable, and they are helping me breathe.

The half marathon begins, and the adrenaline carries me for a few miles. The event itself is amazing because along the course there are musicians playing, bands performing, and locals present to cheer you along. I find it weirdly emotional. It turns out running for a purpose bigger than yourself is way better than running just so you don't feel bad about all the Popeyes you intend to eat later.

As for my goals, I'm two out of three. I obviously don't die, and, much to my joy, I don't finish last, but I definitely walk in certain spots. Do you not remember me saying I'd only run five miles in preparation? Of course I walk some.

I don't know if this half marathon in any way prepared me to be a better parent, but I do know that being forced to reckon with my nature as a person and, even more, to reconsider that nature was a lesson I needed to learn so that one day I could teach it. Isn't that what parenting is: helping your kids learn lessons earlier than you did so that they can avoid your failures (or at the very least, experience them early enough so you can help them turn those failures into educational foundations)?

I had to force myself to find pride in just completing the race. It will never be said that I set any speed records in that particular half marathon, but *I did it*, and that's a pretty apt metaphor for parenting. In a lot of ways, we make parenting into an all-out sprint and build it around heightened moments. But the art of parenting is about a consistent rhythm and steady gait. I'm finding that a lot of it is about showing up and making yourself available and vulnerable, not because you necessarily want to, but because you can't bear the thought of living in a world where your kids needed you for something and instead of being there, you just bailed. It might not be pretty, and it might give you blisters, but what else would you rather be doing?

FOURTEEN

KID NAMES

It feels like unique kid names are having a moment, right? As a species we're more self-aware than we've ever been, and that has translated into us being really intentional about the names of our children. And yeah, sometimes that tips into levels of ridiculousness, but this intentionality also means that the next few generations of kids won't grow up with 89 percent of all men named "John."

Think about it: there are a ton of old guy names that may be on the verge of extinction:

1. Richard[1]
2. Gary
3. Frank
4. Cosby
5. Bert
6. Ernie

---

1. Do I need to explain this? I really want to, but my editors really don't want me to. They want me to Do Intellectually Consider Kindness (do you get it?) on this point, and so I will.

7. Clarence
8. Clyde
9. Gene
10. Harold

Those names are just a few examples of old-white-guy names that are on the cusp of being shelved. The propulsive element behind this shelving is a sort of parental vanity attached to names nowadays, something Ashley and I are very much a part of.

When we found out that Ashley was pregnant with our second child and that this child would be a girl, we immediately began brainstorming names. We knew we wanted something beautiful but also unique, and the one we landed with proved to be beautiful but also complicated: Sidda Gray. In naming her this, we knew that odds were good that she would never have to encounter someone else with a name like hers. But along with this comes a generic period of understanding required upon learning her name.

We get it, because her name is slightly different, though it's not truly bizarre like Motorcade Benevolence Prospector McCoy. Still, we get a lot of questions about the origin of her name. While Ashley feels compelled to rationalize our choice, I don't. In matters of personal choice, I live by the credo "Only God can judge me."

To me, there are two kinds of interactions: meaningful/authentic and proximity-imposed. For interactions with people that happen only because of your locus, none of what you say really matters, does it? I cannot emphasize this enough. I mean, you need to be good and decent and humane, but you aren't under oath to spill all your secrets as accurately as possible just because you happened to be caught in their spiderweb of conversation.

Children are the great equalizer in this situation because stray conversations always seem to trend to kids. But this opens up some land mines, because what's the first thing people usually want to know? Your kid's name. And for us, this always invites the response "Wow, that's . . . different. How'd you come up with that?"

Which is a fine and totally valid question, but remember, I'm not under any obligation to reveal that information. So I lie, and usually I do this by calling her name "a family name." It is 100 percent not a family name, but no one cares about the truth; they just want an explanation, and most people eat the family connection right up.

I truly believe that you could fumble out any name or combination of syllables, but as long as you qualify it with "It's a family name," no one will say a word against it. Dogplate Riflenuts, Adalard Hitlerface, Shmuckpants McZoobleezoo; all of these names are granted conversational acceptance just by associating them to the deep lineage of your family tree.

Look, I'm not here to judge your kids' names. I honestly don't care. My kids have very unique names, so to judge yours would be a very pot-kettle-black situation, and I usually try to avoid those at all costs.

But I do encourage you to reconsider telling people your unborn child's name.

It's a natural impulse. You, the would-be parent, are excited about the new life you will soon be overseeing. Other people, being supportive, observational, and thoughtful, want to share in this process by doing the only thing they can: asking questions.

Which is good, right? Well, yes and no. As you'll see, I'm a very pro-questions kind of guy, but the goodness of the question all depends on its nature. Is it an empty transaction in service to politeness, or is it conceptual to the point of achieving a better, deeper understanding?

Questions about your kids' names are always the former because the only thing people care about when asking about a pregnancy are *their* feelings about it. For example, the questions you normally get asked when you or your partner is pregnant include:

- **Are you excited?** Your answer will tell them that something is wrong because either you aren't excited enough or you are too excited to the point of idiotic naïveté.
- **When is the baby due?** The answer will tell them that the person carrying the baby either has gained entirely too much weight or isn't showing enough, which means it's a vanity issue or incompetent maternal instinct.
- **A stupid rhetorical question about never sleeping well again.** Your answer means nothing. The mere existence of your pregnancy makes them arrogant about their immediate sleeping futures. Hear me on this: there is nothing worse than someone drunk with sleep arrogance.

Again, I'm definitely team questions because questions help identify answers, which lead to a fuller understanding. But some things don't need to be understood. Some things just *are*, like your unborn child's name. And the solidity of that doesn't need more understanding by someone who isn't you. Because—and this is the thesis of the whole chapter—for you, the name is chosen. It is perfect, God-breathed, and inerrant, and once you lock it in, it's less a choice and more a manifestation of something that always was and always will be.

But this is not at all true to other people. To understand this, it's important to recognize the disparity of emotional investment in this equation. To you, your baby is your literal flesh and blood, but to them, it's still an Inaccessible Idea. It's the whisper of a ghost, and that ghost is named Liam, or Kyle, or Phoebe because you loved the show *Friends*. But this is complicated because they always hated *Friends* and found the song "Smelly Cat" to not even be that clever.

Think about it: even in the best-case scenario, if you reveal your unborn child's name, the person will either tacitly endorse it, leaving you underwhelmed and somewhat questioning of the choice, or endorse it so enthusiastically that you will see right through their charade of fake support. And remember, I said this was the *best*-case scenario.

In a worst-case scenario, the person will outright lampoon the name and relate some unfortunate anecdote about a kid they grew up with who had the same name and suffered from some bizarrely specific and humiliating identifier, thereby brandishing your unborn child with this unfortunate identifier for eternity.

EXAMPLE:

YOU

We're naming him Samuel.

THEM

Gross. Samuel?

YOU

(emotionally devastated and already questioning the monogramming spree

95

you've gone on) Yeah, what's wrong with
Samuel?

THEM

I don't know. I always think of Samuel
from my fourth-grade class. He had
skin tags, so everyone just called him
Skin Tag Sam.

YOU

Oh.

THEM

Anyways, wanna go to Buffalo Wild Wings?

Prior to the birth of our second child, my first daughter, I
loved the name Emerson. It felt like a cool confluence of masculine and feminine names, and it was also extremely literary,
which is an English-major consideration that people like me can't
get away from. But the name was back-burnered forever after the
following exchange.

FRIEND

Have you zeroed in on any names yet?

ME

I really love Emerson.

FRIEND

Emerson?

ME

Yeah, do you like it?

FRIEND

Really? Emerson if it's a girl? Really?

ME

Yes, why are you saying it like that?

FRIEND

You've never thought of boys teasing her with "Emerson big ole boobies?"

ME

(utterly and comprehensively speech-less) Why . . . on planet Earth . . . why would I have ever thought of this scenario?

FRIEND

You have to think of these things when naming girls, my dude. Anyways, wanna go to Buffalo Wild Wings?

Our eight-year-old daughter has already warned us that maybe she doesn't want to be identified with a double name. "Sidda Gray" is a mouthful for friends (and as it turns out, an intellectual mouthful for some adults), so she's considering just being Sidda. And that's okay with us, because it's her name and she has to live with it, so she might as well enjoy what it is.

Any awkward interactions about her name have never once made me reconsider our choice. But I am aware that while the name my daughter bears is the one we gave her, it's up to her to keep it, accept it, or change it. Because beyond representing our identity, our names represent the battle to balance who we are, where we come from, and who we want to be.

FIFTEEN

HOME

I'm sitting in my car in a parking lot. My door is open, and I'm patiently waiting to vomit.

It's a Target parking lot, to be precise. And while that might conjure up notions of fancifulness or a preface to retail bliss, this is definitely not that, for a lot of reasons.

First, I've been to this Target before, and while it is technically a Super Target, that "Super" designation is in name only. If we're being honest, this Target is busted, and if you frequent Target or hold it in high regard, there's nothing worse than a busted Target.

Busted Targets and busted Chick-fil-As are a particular kind of Paradise Lost, because you approach them expecting a certain experience, and when you don't get it, the effect is jarring (what was versus what could have been, etc.).

At this specific Target the employees are 10 percent grouchier than normal, and there are always 95 percent fewer checkout lanes open than there should be regardless of the crowd.[1]

---

1. I'm throwing numbers around as though I've used some kind of formula to arrive at these figures, but why bring data to a feelings-fest, you know what I'm saying?

I'm belaboring the point, but you get it: this Target sucks. But that honestly has nothing to do with why I'm in the parking lot about to toss a sidewalk pizza.[2]

I don't even plan to go into the Target at all. I've chosen this specific parking lot because it is set back amid a sea of other brick-and-mortar behemoths such as Best Buy, World Market, and Buffalo Wild Wings.[3] And mainly I've chosen it because I know I'm going to vomit, and if I have to vomit in public, I want to do it in a mostly empty parking lot so no one can see me.

As to the context around this unfortunate reality, I've been en route to see the home we're buying in a move that will take our family from Tennessee to Alabama. But I got a phone call telling me that everything has fallen through—our approval to buy the house and our plans to move away. After months spent reconsidering what home really means, we have to immediately reconsider where our home will be.

Even as a kid, I was never someone to have natural pride in where I'm from. It's not that I'm too cool for something like that or openly hostile to my geographic roots. It just seemed strange to subjectively lionize a location just because it happened to have my presence within its borders.

That's not to say that I won't always have a fondness for Tennessee; I definitely will, but I have a weird way of allowing

---

2. That means "throw up." Could you figure that out or did you need this footnote? It's for sure a very indulgent way to relate the idea of vomiting, but I still love it.
3. Real quick: Smooch/Marry/Kill those retail establishments. I'll go smooch Best Buy, marry World Market, and kill Buffalo Wild Wings.

emotions and fondness for something to creep in only after my experience is over.

I remember the first time I reconsidered the expectations that come alongside living in a specific place. I was eight years old, and my reconsideration was connected to the unspoken obligation to root for the Tennessee Volunteers. In Tennessee there's an outsized adulation for the University of Tennessee because for many years it was the only significant conduit of sports in the state. In my childhood the Tennessee Titans were still in Houston and the Memphis Grizzlies were still in Vancouver. And you could argue that many Tennesseans wouldn't really be that heartbroken if both teams returned from whence they came.[4]

Because of that, the University of Tennessee in Knoxville was the sports epicenter of the state, and the various Volunteer teams shouldered the hopes and dreams of most Tennesseans. But I wasn't really feeling it. The Volunteers wore a shade of orange that is best described as painfully orange, though not as painful as the university fight song, "Rocky Top," which could have been used in *Zero Dark Thirty* as a torture technique superior to testicular electrocution.

In my heart I wanted to root for the Florida State Seminoles. They played crazy good defense, their offense was explosive, and most of all, before every game their mascot—a Native American playing the part of Chief Osceola—rode out to the fifty-yard line and spiked a flaming spear onto the field.[5] This was in the top five of coolest things I'd ever seen, just behind all of *Jurassic*

---

4. *Hamilton* reference.
5. I just want to emphasize that this was the '90s, and I was unaware that appropriating Native American culture for sports entertainment was not great.

Park and just ahead of what happens when you put Mentos into a Diet Coke.

What I was realizing then, and have since understood even more deeply, is that sometimes the place you feel most at home is far away from where you are.

Until Ashley and I decided to move, I'd never considered what home meant beyond the physical definition. For thirty-four years I'd lived within the same twenty-mile radius of southeast Tennessee (excepting one year of college at Samford University), and this was less a choice than it was an inherited reality. And just as you don't feel the same connection for something you are given versus something you choose and earn, I never felt much of a connection to Tennessee.

As do any people uprooting their lives and family, once Ashley and I decided to leave, we received a lot of questions about why we were moving. For us, the process of deciding to move was simultaneously a long time coming and very abrupt. We briefly entertained moving away every year or so, but it never made sense.

Through it all, we always lingered on Birmingham as a viable option since it wasn't too far away from our families. Plus I'd lived there in college and loved it. It's an incredible place with a lot of deeply personal meaning to me.

Starting a business online with my friend Jamie Golden enhanced my affinity for the city. She and our first hire, Erin Moon, both lived there. Everything seemed to be coming up Birmingham, and this heightened what was beginning to feel like a disconnect with where we lived in Tennessee.

Have you ever lived in a place for a long time but felt like no one knew you? That might be a familiar and universal thing, or it could just be a trope of young adult literature. At any rate, that's what Tennessee felt like to Ashley and me. We'd been there our whole lives, and we'd gotten to the point that we couldn't differentiate which relationships and friendships were actively chosen by us and which ones were just the result of shared proximity.

We loved the familiarity we had with where we lived, but it began to feel oppressive—especially in contrast with the unfamiliarity I was experiencing in both who I was as a person and what I believed. All of this crescendoed with an overwhelming sense of our lives being a mishmash of "just because."

My beliefs were just because.

Our lives were just because.

Where we lived was just because.

Everything was just because.

A year prior to actually moving, we'd pushed to make Birmingham happen. We'd looked at houses and had even found someone to buy our house in Tennessee without having to list it, but the timing just didn't feel right, and we couldn't find peace with it. We agreed to table the idea completely and forever because our kids were getting old enough that a move could destabilize their social relationships.

But a year later, unbeknownst to each other, the desire to move returned to each of us. Despite agreeing to table this conversation and despite making plans to put roots down in our Tennessee home, the feeling was vivid for both of us.

My many years in church surrounded me with people whose instinct would be to call this desire "a God thing" or "the Spirit" or "God's calling." But I'm well aware how we can finesse our desires to appear like God's, so I'll stop short of putting that kind of a rubber stamp on this feeling we shared.

Suffice it to say, maybe God really was moving in our hearts, or maybe we just really wanted to go and therefore repackaged our ambition into a divine orchestration. I don't know that anyone can ever properly disentangle these two elements. But we were both secretly and individually praying and thinking about the possibility of moving, and one night this twin deception was revealed.

INT. KITCHEN—EVENING

The kids are in bed. Knox and Ashley haven't eaten dinner yet. Knox looks carefully at three different takeout menus spread on the island counter.

KNOX

Where's your head at?

ASHLEY

I'm afraid to say.

KNOX

Why?

ASHLEY

I don't think you are going to like it.

HOME

KNOX

You might be surprised. Let's just count
to three and say what we're thinking.

ASHLEY

Okay.

KNOX

One, two, three.

KNOX

Chinese food.

ASHLEY

I think we should move to Birmingham.

(A brief silence overtakes the room.)

ASHLEY

I know last year we said we were done
with thinking about Birmingham, but I
just can't stop thinking about it.

KNOX

I can't either. I can't believe you've
been thinking about this too.

ASHLEY

I know, right?

(A pregnant pause. They are both silently bonded by the almost supernaturally timed revelation and what this might mean for their futures.)

KNOX

And while I definitely want to keep this convo going, we do need to make a decision on dinner. I think Chinese is what I was hearing?

Following this conversation, we set specific requirements of what it would take for us to move. Part of this was because of the realities of life like finding new schools for our kids, which would quickly become untenable if we left the window to move open for too long. But the unspoken intention of these requirements was to be a sort of hypothesis testing of God. It was almost our way of saying to God, "All right, let's see if you really want us to move."

We gave it forty days. In forty days we had to sell our house, find one to move into, and have closings scheduled. If we couldn't, there was no need for further action,[6] as that would be our answer, no takebacks.

As it turned out, we sold our house in fifteen days at our list price, and we found a house to buy a few days after that. Whether it was God or a hot real estate market I didn't know, but I *did* know that our hypothetical reconsideration of home was now a tangible thing.

The weeks that followed were hard. We had to contend with

---

6. *Hamilton* reference.

not only all the moving parts (nailed it) and red tape of real estate but also the emotionality of our decision. After all, this choice wasn't affecting just Ashley and me; it was affecting our kids, our parents, our extended family, and the intertwinings of how all those relationships were going to change now that we weren't a few minutes away. In truth, this was and forever will be the hardest part of leaving.

Back in the Crappy Target parking lot, I'm not vomiting because I'm sick; I'm vomiting because I'm terrified. It's one of very few times in my life that I've felt helpless and out of options. Suddenly all our momentum is gone, and I just don't understand. We tested the God hypothesis and the most difficult boxes have been checked. We emotionally, spiritually, and mentally prepared to leave, and we're days away from loading our entire home into a moving truck. And now is when we get our stop sign?

To be honest, I feel frustrated with God. But even more honestly, I wonder if God hasn't factored into our equation at all, and our move is something borne from selfish discontent, and now we are finally getting our proper comeuppance.

We started this entire process wanting to reconsider home, but now it is all too much.

But a few minutes post-vomit, my bank's mortgage specialist calls and relays that he's been mistaken. He submitted the wrong data for final approval. The house I've been on my way to see will soon become our home, a vomit-stop detour notwithstanding.

I've gotten really good at carving out different manifestations of home for myself. Not in the literal sense of a physical structure around me but in the metaphorical sense of places where I find comfort, familiarity, and acceptance. And while these things are uniformly good, homes are meant to be left so we can return to the truest sense of what they are. To me, the perfect mystery of home is that you have to leave it to properly appreciate it.

SIXTEEN

BIG BIRD

"Why is Big Bird called Big Bird?"

My daughter asked me this recently while we were watching TV.

I grew up with *Sesame Street* just as you probably grew up with *Sesame Street*. Everyone there is ageless and exists on a space-time continuum uninfluenced by external events. The characters exist in a sort of cultural purgatory, but in a good way, as if the internet was never invented and the impending doom of climate change isn't bearing down on them like it is on us.

Every now and again, my kids will skate across *Sesame Street* and be entertained by it for a moment before skipping onward, imprisoned by their corrupted attention spans. But when they do hang around, it's usually because of the presence of Big Bird, which I get because Big Bird is big, yellow, and a bird. He's very consistent with the template laid out by his name.

But the weird thing about Big Bird is that the more you look into Big Bird, the more unsettling the character becomes.

I know what you are thinking: Big Bird is a lovable, giant

bird with vivid yellow feathers, and he has a vulnerable affability that makes him both distinct and approachable. What could be unsettling about that? Nothing, really, unless you reconsider why it is that we're asked to refer to Big Bird as "Big."

When I was a child, before my dad started his own business, he worked for a man we will call Jerry. As it so happened, Jerry had a son my age, and we often played together. This child's name was also Jerry. To differentiate between them, adult Jerry was called "Big Jerry" and the child Jerry was called "Little Jerry." This was helpful nomenclature, and it was so effective that it remains in practice even though Big Jerry passed away several years ago. If my parents ever relate an update or piece of news about the child Jerry, he's still referred to as Little Jerry.

Let's consider this in relation to Big Bird. Off the top of your head, are you aware of any other birds on *Sesame Street*? While minor bird characters have visited before, they are not regular players and don't appear enough to presumably have any kind of residence or social standing there.

So I return to my daughter's original question: Why is Big Bird called Big Bird?

We can't call it a nickname because typically, nicknames are not a reflection of reality as that defeats the fun of a nickname.

So what kind of Big Mob-Boss Mood possesses someone to demand that others refer to them with the qualifier "Big" when simply "Bird" would do? It's weirdly specific, no?

Even more, if we were to allow Big Bird the indulgence of self-identifying with a bit of razzle-dazzle, wouldn't the move be to "Yellow Bird"?

Why "Big Bird"?

I have a few theories:

1. Big Bird is fixated on status and the subconscious influ-ence of reiterating his size over the other citizens of Sesame Street.
2. He didn't choose the designation "Big Bird" as much as he inherited it from those he had victimized.
3. It's a vestigial identifier left over from a time when Sesame Street was teeming with bird life, and now Big Bird wears the name as a mournful reminder of his genus's eventual extinction.
4. Perhaps a species war broke out on Sesame Street, and Big Bird betrayed his kind in exchange for status and suprem-acy after the battle.

Speculations abound, but we'll never know the real truth around why Big Bird insists on the superfluous qualifier. I tried explaining the depth of this intricacy to my child who originated the query, but early into my explanation, her attention span got the best of her. She'd moved on to *Shimmer and Shine*, a show about two sister genies who live happily and contentedly in a bottle, a suspicious premise if I've ever heard one.

SEVENTEEN

BEDTIME

If you have kids, you know that the greatest battles of human history happen nightly between emotionally worn-down parents and their somehow-untired children. Ali had Frazier. Mario had Bowser. Holmes had Moriarty, and O. J. had legality, but the biggest conflicts occur between parents and kids who just don't want to go to bed. (And if you don't have kids, just keep this fact in your heart or something. It's good context for what we're about to talk about.)

Bedtime is a struggle for Ashley and me. For me, schedules are a kind of god to be observed, yes, but more appropriately to be worshipped by our adherence to them. For Ashley, time is fluid and schedules are like a choose-your-own-adventure setup. Why schedule when you can be spontaneous?

But even if we were completely aligned on the schedule front, the reality about parenting is that getting a child to bed is incredibly difficult. It's truly the climactic struggle in, depending on your kids' ages, a day full of struggles.

Somehow children get stronger throughout the day despite

physically and emotionally always being dialed up to ten, and their resolve is never more powerful than it is when you are directing them toward the finality of bedtime. This is significant because for a lot of parents, post-bedtime is often the only mental respite a day can offer.

Ashley and I divide the day between BB (Before Bedtime) and AB (After Bedtime). AB is particularly important for us because this is the only time we can sit with and catch up with each other without fear of interruption, intersibling conflict mediation, or juice requests. Accordingly, we look forward to this time, and thus our resolve is hardened the closer we get to it. This in turn clashes with our children's already hardened resolves not to go to bed, setting the stage for a situation that has the same energy as Gerard Butler from *300*.

But the weird thing about having kids is that the second you're away from them, you start to kind of miss them. This absence is heightened by our complete awareness that time is fleeting and we have to make every moment count.

Parents have always known this, by the way. That isn't a new development or discovery; it's just that mass media is now emotionally bullying us with this idea. There are sappy commercials and social media infographics to batter us across the face with the realization that every second that ticks off the clock is one second closer to pretty much all the sad things.

We're one second closer to another Star Wars movie that everyone is going to see but still endlessly complain about.[1]

We're one second closer to the invariable BuzzFeed article

---

1. People, it's Star Wars. Remember when the prequels came out and they were all Jar Jar Binks? Now we have Rey, Finn, Kylo, and Poe. There's even a ball-shaped droid named BB-8. Why so serious?

proving that ice cream causes elbow cancer. That's definitely going to be a harrowing day.

We're one second closer to the revelation that the pig who played Babe in the movie *Babe* was inappropriate to all the other farm animals.

But the unsubtle text to all of this is that we're one second closer to our kids not just leaving for college but getting to the point where they don't need us to tuck them in anymore. Or their hangout preferences are stacked with people who are definitely not us. This doesn't seem like the end of the world when you've just been asked to watch your child do a cannonball into the pool for the eighty-four-thousandth time, but when the realization arrives that I didn't carpe my parenting diem as much as I could have, I can guarantee that I will ugly cry worse than I did after *Toy Story 3* and *4*.

Simultaneously trying to be appropriately selfish while also living up to some unachievable parental ideal that only exists in pharmaceutical commercials is enough to give you whiplash.[2] Needless to say, it's almost impossible to perfectly thread that parental needle, and I myself am often exceedingly inconsistent in my approach to bedtime.

In the fifteen minutes before bedtime, I rule our home with an iron fist and bark with the authority of a drill sergeant. But fifteen minutes after the kids have been in bed? I develop the soul of a poet and miraculously become an advocate of free-range bedtime.

Obviously, I need to try to strike a balance, but how is that even possible? Everything I see and read emphasizes structure

---

2. Seriously though, have you ever seen more perfectly idyllic people than the ones that exist in pharmaceutical commercials? But think about it: they have to be perfectly idyllic because the picture of some old guy fly fishing in Montana with his forty-eight grandchildren distracts us from hearing that the medicine featured in this ad may have side effects including infinite bloody diarrhea insomnia.

and consistency—and that is legit the sweetest sweet music to my structured ears—but there has to be some nuance there, right? How are we supposed to carpe diem if the only time we're encouraged to do so is when it's scheduled and blocked off between lacrosse practices and playdates?

Thus, I can easily be swayed to ditch convention and routine in pursuit of a bigger experience.

For example, a few months ago I was cleaning out my car in the garage after getting the kids to bed. We were leaving for a trip later that week, so I wanted order and cleanliness in the car in advance of leaving—a fool's errand if there ever was one.

I'd left the garage door open because the night was quiet and dark, and the weather alternated between horror-movie fog and the kind of drizzly mist-rain that makes you want to stare out a window and monologue about your sorrows.

I finished vacuuming the back seat and turned around to look outside only to find my son standing just outside the garage door like a pint-sized Jason Voorhees.

And can I just say that when kids are up past bedtime, they take on a new posture that is some combination of sneaky, creepy, and mischievous.[3] They absolutely know that what they are doing is unsanctioned, so the entire time they are up, they're just waiting to get busted. They kind of just linger, not exactly hiding but not exactly not hiding either. It's very missysneakcreepvious.[4]

So you understand that, when I saw my son, my instinctual reaction was to quietly say, "S-word."[5]

---

3. Missysneakcreepvious? I think I love that word.

4. Again, love this word. It's really growing on me.

5. I am afforded no expletives in this book, so I'm handling my truth the best way I can. Thank you for your thoughts and prayers in this difficult time.

Not because I was mad or because I routinely say the s-word. And not even because I wanted to say the s-word with a heightened seriousness. No, I said it because he genuinely startled me, and sometimes when you are unexpectedly frightened, you just have to say the s-word to get through a situation. I don't know what else to really tell you about that. (Like you wouldn't also say "s-word" if you turned around to see what looks like a supernatural presence staring at you in a darkened garage after 10:00 p.m.? Honestly, I bet "s-word" is tame compared to what some of you would say. Animals.)

Anyways, my bedtime drill-sergeant mentality immediately kicked in. My internal monologue went toward, *Now I have to stop what I'm doing and get him back to bed because it's super late, and if he doesn't get enough rest, he won't wake up easily and getting to school on time will be impossible, and if we don't get him to school on time, I might be late for a meeting in Atlanta* . . .

I could see the chain of events leading to a stressful day tomorrow, and I was already starting to get anxious about how the damage was already done and our lives were all basically ruined forever. But then I was interrupted out of my anxiety by my son asking me a profound question:

"What does 's-word' mean?"

How do you explain what the s-word means to a six-year-old without indicting your parental malfeasance? Even if you could morally fall on your sword and manage to get to the point where you are trying to define an expletive, how can you define all the different iterations of the s-word? It really is such a rich text.

- It's something you say in response to frustration or unexpected complication.

- It's a word that generalizes physical stuff.
- It's a word that generalizes emotional stuff.
- It's another word for poop.

And sometimes it's something you say when you realize you're missing the bigger picture. And in that moment I was missing it, and I knew this because I had been missing it for a while.

See, when you are addicted to routine, you never reconsider what exists in the margins. And even more, what you are missing. You get kind of puritanical about your fidelity to structure, and to even consider what you could be doing is tantamount to chaos. But sometimes we all need to do a trust fall into a little chaos.

I skipped the vocab lesson and instead asked my son what he was up to. He said, "Nothing, really." He was just curious if we could throw the football around for a little bit.

It was long after 10:00 p.m. and this was a bad idea for a million reasons—the ones I laid out earlier and so many more. Also, this was just bad precedent. And wasn't this going to rile him up? He'd definitely get sweaty before bed, and who in the world can sleep when they're sweaty? The pros and cons list for this idea was decisively heavy on the cons.

But we threw the football anyway.

Not because I'm a great parent—do you not remember that I said the s-word in front of him?—but because it felt like something he might remember. And for that reason alone, it felt worth doing, for both of our sakes.

EIGHTEEN

MIDDAY NAPS

There's a lot of evidence pointing to midday naps being an inherently good idea:

- Kids do it.
- It's sleeping.
- It's a cultural fixture throughout European countries and beyond.

Beyond that, a cursory internet search will turn up no less than eleven hundred million thousand life hack articles about how a twelve-minute nap can change your life.

Clearly the lobbying fingerprints of Big Nap are all over this push, because no reasonable, average person can regularly nap, much less in twelve-minute increments. A regular, midday nap is the most luxurious of luxuries, and it seems about as realistic as any book promising to help you have a single-digit-hour workweek.

In a lot of ways, the myth of the short, daily nap was like the evangelical myth I grew up with that claimed everyone in church was doing a twenty-minute daily devotion. Maybe I'm wrong on this (LOL, I'm not), but the presented vibe was that everyone was always spending quiet time with their Bibles, inspirational journals, and a seventeen-pack of highlighters—when a very small minority, if any, actually were.

Which is why I want to reconsider it. Not because sleeping in the middle of the day is an inherently bad thing, but because it does not seem compatible with your standard workday schedule.

Is this *Mad Men*'s fault? Did they bring napping back? Are they to blame for this nap-aissance? If you watched the show, you know that while characters like Don Draper definitely napped during the day, exactly none of those people were in healthy emotional or personal places.

Who started this rumor that we live in a world where our jobs allow us to randomly nap? And even if they did, like we could achieve slumber in a cubicle that smells like Jimmy John's and essential oils? Sha' right.

I don't know about you, but my body just isn't built for napping. When I sleep, I go big. Closed eyes, full REM cycles, can't lose, etc. So to have to go in and out of that in twelve, twenty, or even thirty minutes? It's just not happening. Especially not if you expect me to engage competently on a conference call post-nap.

And look, I'm not naïve. I know there are people who can nap effectively. These people are probably even doing stuff like micronapping, where you fall asleep for thirty-eight seconds. If that's you, just know that I pretty much loathe you.

If you are someone who can nap regularly in the middle of the day, don't ever tell anyone, because the only people who can nap like that without judgment are new mothers. That's the literal only chance they have left, so you go, girl. Otherwise, tell no one because the world will hate you for it.

It's a similar plight to that of an X-Man or X-Woman. Or the kind of person who can sit naturally on a chaise lounge. Or the kind of person who can confidently use a bidet and pronounces the word *mature* like "ma-tour." The rest of the world resents and fears you because they don't understand you.

Sure, naps are okay if you are jet-lagged or have a free Sunday to yourself, but let's completely reconsider the mirage that you need to have a midafternoon nap from 2:24 p.m. to 2:36 p.m. to be your most productive self.

NINETEEN

LEBRON JAMES VS. MICHAEL JORDAN

Before I began applying the exercise of reconsideration across all boundaries of my life, the most existential reconsideration I undertook involved figuring out who is the greatest basketball player of all time.

Every major sport broadly assigns an owner of the title "Greatest of All Time," and the NBA is no different. I was prompted to ponder who holds that title in basketball when my son asked me out of mild curiosity. However, his question did present a bit of a pickle.

It would have been easy to just say, "My beloved child, Michael Jordan is the greatest basketball player to ever live." This would appease his curiosity and arm him with a certainty and an easy alliance with conventional wisdom that would rarely get challenged in social situations.

But it wouldn't be correct. And shouldn't that matter?

Eventually, you have to choose principle over ease of

understanding, even if the issue at hand is of little consequence. That's why I told my son that LeBron James is the best basketball player ever—and the competition really isn't close.

Usually those who believe MJ to be the best point to his six championships as an unassailable and impenetrable fortress of his GOATness. To be clear, championships are pretty important, especially when it comes to basketball. When you have the smallest group of players contributing to the success of your team as opposed to every other major team sport, each individual's involvement is force-multiplied. This cannot be understated.

When it has been mathematically determined that MJ's six rings are superior to LeBron's three rings, most people think the issue has been settled. But that's actually when the conversation is just getting started. Because if you are going to look at championships, you have to look at the context around those championships, right? When we do that, a much more complicated picture emerges.

For example, exactly none of MJ's championship season titles were won from the position of underdog. His Bulls team was the heavy favorite in every finals appearance. Said a little differently, MJ never ran into a superior opponent or a superior collection of talent when he made it into the finals. Perhaps even more importantly, when you study all of his finals opponents, the teams fall into one of two categories: Talented But Inexperienced or Trending Toward Decline.

For example, we could label the '91 Los Angeles Lakers as a TTD team because they were a (mostly) skeleton crew of stars led by an aging Magic Johnson, who only months later would retire after testing positive for HIV. Similarly, the '92 Portland Trail Blazers, also a TTD team, had an overmatched Clyde Drexler and not much else.

The '93 Phoenix Suns were a TBI team in that they had the MVP Charles Barkley, but they also lacked significant amounts of postseason experience. To be fair, this was the most talented team MJ would contend with, and they were very, very good.

But in 1994, just as this Suns team and a Houston Rockets juggernaut were ascending in the Western Conference, a young rookie named Shaquille O'Neal was ascending in Jordan's own Eastern Conference. Then Jordan retired to play baseball.[1] Jordan took off most of 1995 as well and returned too late in the season to create any real momentum. His Bulls were eliminated by a precocious Orlando Magic team led by O'Neal and Penny Hardaway. Obviously, it isn't fair to count this failure against him though.

Reinvigorated, MJ returned in full force in 1996, and his Bulls met the Seattle SuperSonics in the finals. The Sonics were talented; they featured Gary Payton, defensive specialist and trash-talker supreme, and Shawn Kemp, a ferocious dunker with an even more ferocious appetite who was just two years away from almost eating himself out of the league. But despite being talented and having great multiseason win totals, the team hadn't yet made it out of the first round of the playoffs prior to this appearance.

For the remainder of his finals appearances, Jordan faced off with the Utah Jazz, a formidable but classic TTD team featuring the past-their-primes duo of John Stockton and Karl Malone.

Not only were Jordan's opponents lacking, but they were also significantly outmanned, since the Chicago Bulls' supporting cast around Jordan was a veritable Death Star of talent.

---

1. By "retired to play baseball," I mean that I subscribe to the theory that MJ was asked to step away from the NBA by commissioner David Stern after being implicated in several different gambling scandals. This was done to help the NBA avoid a situation that the MLB had endured a few years earlier after Pete Rose was found to have been betting on baseball games while managing the Cincinnati Reds.

It's unfair to dock Jordan points because his team roster featured specialists specifically chosen to complement his talents. Or because he played alongside another one of the top twenty players of all time in Scottie Pippen, and under perhaps the greatest NBA coach of all time. But we're also obligated not to let those variables go unmentioned when painting the larger picture around Jordan's accomplishments. Were they great? Obviously. But does the confluence of all these harmonious factors prove that he is the greatest of all time? To me, it does not.

Going back to the subject of opponents in the finals, you could argue that LeBron James has never been favored in any of his matchups. The weakest year for this argument was 2011, his first year with the Heat, when they squared off against Dirk Nowitzki and the Dallas Mavericks.

LeBron was playing on a new team with Dwyane Wade and Chris Bosh, while the Mavericks were a seasoned roster replete with capable and complementary role players with an assortment of finals experience. The widespread belief was that the Heat were better, but on paper it was a much more compelling matchup because LeBron's team was a classic iteration of the TBI teams.

After that year, though, LeBron faced off against the dynastic San Antonio Spurs two times, the dynastic Golden State Warriors four times, and an Oklahoma City Thunder team that had three future league MVPs in James Harden, Kevin Durant, and Russell Westbrook.

Against these stacked circumstances, LeBron managed three titles, the crown jewel of which is the iconic comeback after being down three games to one in the 2016 NBA Finals. This culminated in LeBron chasing down Andre Iguodala and pinning his shot against the backboard, leading to Kyrie Irving's go-ahead three that would eventually prove to be the deciding shot in upsetting the outrageously favored Warriors. This achievement is significant because LeBron's Cavaliers team is the only one to ever come back from such a deficit. In doing so LeBron managed to sully the Warriors' record-breaking year in which they shattered the regular-season wins record that had been held by—wait for it—Jordan's 1996 Chicago Bulls.

Additionally, Jordan never faced the centralized mobilization of the league against his efforts as LeBron has faced every single year of his prime. Since LeBron entered the league, his teams and situations have commanded the focus of every other team in a way that Jordan never had to endure. This is partially because in the '90s the league didn't have player empowerment as it does now. But it's also because the league then just didn't orbit Jordan like the NBA has orbited LeBron for almost fifteen years.

To me the biggest and most underrated element to consider is the disparity with which each player entered the league. Michael Jordan was chosen third overall in the 1984 NBA Draft behind Hakeem Olajuwon and Sam Bowie. While third overall isn't too shabby, for Jordan it was yet another affront of underestimation, now numerous in his origin story. This origin story also involves being cut from his high school basketball team (a story he commemorated by pettily inviting that same coach to his Hall of Fame induction and then excoriating him in front of everyone). These slights, however faint they might be, contribute to our perception of Jordan as an avenging basketball prodigy. They are a sort of gasoline fueling his anger and drive, and we romanticize this.

LeBron's path was completely different but just as fascinating. As a junior in *high school* he was featured on the cover of *Sports Illustrated* and declared a lottery pick two years before he was eligible. His high school games were telecast in prime time—on ESPN. And when he was finally available to be drafted, right out of high school, he was chosen first overall. Four years later he had the Cavs in the finals with a coach who, at best, will always be a footnote in other people's stories and with a roster starring players like Larry Hughes, Boobie Gibson, and Scot Pollard.

Whereas Jordan was a routinely misunderstood prodigy who was able to leverage this misrecognition into self-sustaining rage, the entire world knew who and what LeBron was when he was still learning how to drive a car. That has to matter for something, right? It's someone who is exactly who we thought he was (and even more) versus someone who uses others' collective misunderstanding to motivate a leveling-up. The latter, while admirable, does suggest a significant difference in caliber.

Even more, LeBron accepted this burden and carried it capably, despite the obvious "heavy lies the head who wears the crown" complications unique to his career coinciding with the rise of social media. This aspect cannot be overstated enough. LeBron's generation of athletes were the first to coexist with the lens of social media, and we will never know to what extent this intensified the experience of being a professional athlete. Suffice it to say it's definitely had a compounding effect.

But even with this added layer, LeBron has never been in trouble, and he's always been mindful of how his appeal transcends basketball or even what he wants for himself.

In fact, the only real moment when we can collectively agree that LeBron screwed up was in the televising of his decision to sign with the Miami Heat over his hometown Cleveland Cavaliers. It was a tone-deaf public breakup, but it was one constructed with the understanding that all the proceeds from the airing (which ended up being $3 million) would go to the Boys & Girls Clubs of America.

Let's juxtapose this with MJ. He frequently got into fights with teammates, publicly gambled and womanized, and once said that he wanted to stay out of politics because Democrats and Republicans both buy underwear. Again, the times were different so it's not fair to prosecute Jordan for playing in an era when athletes were expected to mostly stick to sports. But it does mean we can reward LeBron for the graceful way in which he's traveled a public landscape that is infinitely more fraught with challenges than anything Jordan ever had to endure.

In the final tallying of who is the basketball greatest of all time, for me it comes down to results on the floor plus degree of difficulty plus cultural impact. And in all of these metrics LeBron is far and away more accomplished than Jordan.

My opinion is a minority one, to be sure. But as passionate as my belief is in the objective greatness of LeBron over MJ, it begs a more interesting conversation about whether we can ever truly mitigate the influences of nostalgia and recency bias in our reconsiderations and pursuit of truth. I'm fortunate in that I was alive for the primes of both MJ and LeBron, so I can't comment on which compulsion is more powerful, the trustworthiness of memory versus the desire to be an eyewitness to the exploits of the greatest ever to play.

A uniquely American quality is that we love to crown new heroes just so we can tear them down, with the hope of eventually building them back up (see Tiger Woods). But in this sense LeBron's greatest victory wasn't against the Warriors in 2016, as I previously stated. It's how in all this time he's never once given us the chance to build him back up—because he was never torn down in the first place.

TWENTY

·

SPORTS TEAMS

When I was six, my parents took me to my first professional baseball game to see the Atlanta Braves play. This was particularly special because the Braves were hosting the Chicago Cubs, my favorite team at the time.[1] The Cubs were my favorite because our TV package got WGN and because Wrigley Field didn't have lights yet in the late '80s, so all their home games were on during the day after school and before bedtime. I watched almost all their games and loved the team, even above the geographically closer Braves.

Early in the game, the Braves began beating the doors off the Cubs, so much so that we left in the sixth inning. And as we did, I sobbed. Not because we were leaving, but because the Cubs were getting waylaid. My tears were made from the kind of anger and indignation that only a six-year-old can summon, but they were also mixed with embarrassment in the sense of, "How could they

---

1. This favoritism would last only a few months more, until I played for the Red Sox as a seven- and eight-year-old and discovered that their stadium had a wall in left field called the Green Monster.

do this to me?" Ryne Sandberg, Mark Grace, Andre Dawson, and Paul Assenmacher[2] had all let me down.

This was a formative experience, but it spoke to a different, deep-seated desire to not be adversely invested in something that didn't deserve it. These seeds of preferring objectivity were sprouting and dovetailing nicely with who I was already becoming, but I could sense a value-proposition imbalance: Why was I expected to care so deeply for a team of loosely confederated and variably motivated people who didn't match my enthusiasm?

Now, as a mostly formed adult, I pride myself on being a pretty objective person. That might sound like a terribly mundane thing to take pride in, but I really do love it.

For one, a worldview defined by objectivity is a fortress against emotions, which feels like the moral high ground. When everyone else around you is losing their minds or taking up inane arguments in the name of supporting something impressive or honorable only because they are emotionally invested in it, my fellow objectives and I get to luxuriate in the satisfaction that comes with seeing the world as it mostly is, not as we want it to be. At this very moment in time, Mitch Trubisky is the quarterback for the Chicago Bears, and he uniformly sucks. Like, so bad. He makes Uncle Rico from *Napoleon Dynamite* look like Tom Brady. By the time you are reading this chapter, he will probably have been supplanted. In this moment that feels very obvious. But in this same moment, there are people who, because they are Bears fans, are trying to talk themselves into Mitch as a viable quarterbacking option. Thus is the plight of invested sports fans.

---

2. Paul Assenmacher was a journeyman middle reliever who will be mostly forgotten— except that you have no idea how fun it was, as a child, to freely say "Assenmacher" without fear of punishment.

And this, combined with my formative experience at Fulton County Stadium in Atlanta, keeps me wondering why we feel so compelled to become die-hard fans, particularly in sports. What is it that makes us feel compelled to root for an arbitrary entity typically under the control of people who are invested for completely different reasons than we are?

That isn't to say that I'm an unemotional automaton who only watches sports for the numerical output variable at the conclusion of each matchup. I regularly get invested, but my investment always becomes about specific people or specific groups of people, or even specific story lines. Emotional, yes, but not a blind, emotional allegiance to teams regardless of who's on them or how they are doing. Even still, I realize that this emotional investment is a rejection of the objectivity I usually abide by, but what can I say? Sometimes it's the flawed humanity that really draws you in.

But as I've gotten older and less tethered to specific institutions or entities, I've watched friends and loved ones get doubly invested. While I understand the tribal/community/membership draw of this, I think it comes at the cost of your agency, which for me is incredibly important to maintain.

My favorite indicator of this loss of agency is when people start to use the word *we* in reference to their favorite teams.

EXAMPLE:

You, just a person at home on your couch watching your favorite team, the Dallas Cowboys: "We've got to increase the tempo and run more play-action."

Did you catch it? Just one word reveals a deeply complicated and unreciprocated relationship. *We* implies that you, just a person at home on your couch, have some kind of feasible connection to the collection of world-class athletes you watch on TV.

But we all know that you don't have any kind of connection, with exceptions being if and only if

- you graduated from the school, or worked or played for the team for at least one year. (None of this "I flunked out of school" or "I would have played for them except that I blew my knee out." Dudes using the excuse of a blown-out knee for why they didn't get a scholarship are only surpassed by white people saying they are some percentage of Native American.)
- you are related to one of the players, coaches, or other active members of the program/organization.
- you donated an obscene amount of money. Tuition money doesn't count, and definitely not if it's an Aunt Becky bribery situation.

This linguistic cleanup is necessary for technical reasons but also for emotional ones. More and more, collegiate sports and professional sports are indicating that there really is no "we," as they only care about their bottom line. That's not an attempt to be populist; it's a reality of the world and how these programs and teams will pay lip service to fan communities when more often than not their fixation is on financial or personal success. And weirdly, I get that. These teams aren't ministries, and as such, I don't have a problem with financial ambition. But the problem comes when these same teams talk out of both sides of their mouths.

- Professional team owners reap massive financial rewards but want local taxpayers to finance their stadiums.

- College coaches parlay their success into better, more high-paying jobs and can leave whenever they like, but the athletes they recruit and promise to coach are encumbered by arcane transfer rules and the coaches' discretion on where they can go.
- When a professional team has to cut or waive a player, it's just "a business decision," but when a player leverages their own freedom or free agency to go elsewhere, it's a "betrayal."
- Universities profit off athletes but deny those same athletes the ability to profit from themselves.[3]

Sports makes for a difficult platform from which to talk about the problem of injustice or hypocrisy because those are the last things we want to align with when enjoying a game, match, or competition. But its tribalistic premise and fandom is predicated on us overlooking those moral inconsistencies. When Tyreek Hill, a wide receiver for the Kansas City Chiefs, is running amok on an opposing defense, sports asks us to forget that in 2014 he choked his pregnant girlfriend and repeatedly punched her in the stomach, and in 2019 he was suspected of battery after his three-year-old son broke his arm.

It's a similarly weird dynamic as when we talk about separating the artist from their art. Did I aesthetically love *House of Cards*? Yes. Does that mean I endorse Kevin Spacey's well-documented problematic behavior? Of course not. I can't go back

---

3. This is probably a conversation for a different book, but the racial optics of not wanting to pay amateur athletes cannot be overlooked. If this was a workforce of white twentysomething young professionals, does anyone really think that they would uniformly be kept from directly profiting from their own likenesses? It would be World War III (sponsored by Brooks Brothers).

and change my feelings of admiration for *House of Cards*, but I can just not think or talk about it anymore. Sports doesn't allow for this distancing because it rewards and mobilizes investment and loyalty. Signed jerseys, tattoos, and basements thematically decorated to testify to your team? Those are the norm. (It would be weird, on the other hand, if my basement was similarly thematically decorated to celebrate Kevin Spacey as Frank Underwood.)

I understand that sports fandom is fundamentally about community and identifying with something larger than yourself, and I respect that. But more and more, we're becoming a migratory population. It's easier to move and relocate, so what does that mean for fandom? Do you always root for a team because one time you lived close to it? Or are you afforded fluidity with who you root for and when you root for them?

This tension is very much at home within the heart of this book, and it speaks to a subtext of discomfort with evolution and change. When confronted with a changing landscape, some of us want to change with it, some of us want to marry elements of change and tradition, and some of us see change as an opportunity to retreat more deeply into who we've always been. Similarly, sports fandom is a vestige of a different time and is now coming to terms with the modern landscape of society and sports.

We have more options now. Instant gratification wasn't our birthright; it just coincided with our existence. The unintended consequence is that the idea of deeply investing in a team that's incompetent, unsuccessful, or both isn't even rational.

Back before the internet, you had to root for the local or regional team because that's all you had access to. But now you have access to everything and everyone. You can watch the local team on the local channel, or you can league pass your way into cities across the country. Yet you're still expected to be betrothed to the same team just because that's who you chose when you were six or that's the team you grew up in geographic proximity to? It makes no sense unless you realize this dynamic is a sort of larger metaphor.

We are born with an inheritance of geography and contexts that typically preconceives and provides what our interpretation of the world will be. This is not necessarily good or bad; it just is. Whether it is about sports, matters of faith, or cilantro as a crucial component in good queso dip,[4] we are conditioned to believe a certain defining philosophy.

But these things are only worth rooting for once they've survived the focus of our considerations as to why we abide by them. I'm not here to say that someone should or should not uniformly adhere to one favorite team, but rather that they should feel the freedom to reconsider their affinity for whomever they root for and the possibility that there is now no more condemnation in not wanting to be shackled to the same team because of regionality. If you want to re-up with your team because you like their color scheme, or the tailgates, or how the games bring your family closer, great. But if you want out from under the historical awfulness of the Washington Redskins, Orlando Magic, or New York Mets, go on and be free.

Because then and only then does it make sense for the failures of someone like Paul Assenmacher[5] to be able to affect us to the point of tears.

---

4. (*Vomits into hands.*)

5. I'm serious: it's legit the most fun name to say bitterly.

PART THREE

RECONSIDER BELIEFS

Believing takes practice.

—MADELEINE L'ENGLE, *A WRINKLE IN TIME*

TWENTY-ONE

UNCLE JOEY

It's hard not to think of *Full House* without smiling fondly. It had a *Three Men and a Baby* vibe, but as a TV show. And instead of just one baby, there were three hysterically cute daughters plus interesting side characters such as Steve, Aunt Becky, and Kimmy Gibbler, as well as a completely perfect golden retriever named Comet. For a certain generation, *Full House* was the most familial of all TV families.

One might argue, though, that it was possibly a little *too* familiar. Allow me to explain.

There has long been this thing that's bugged me about the world in which *Full House* exists: Why did Joey Gladstone hang around so long? It feels like a silly question to ask, right? "Because the plot required him to" is no doubt your reply. And I suppose that could be a satisfactory-enough answer to those who adore simplicity and are eager for the tidiness of fairy-tale stories.

But for me, it wasn't enough. And so I went back to the beginning to examine why Joey came to live in the basement of the Tanners' home in the first place.

We understand that the pilot episode of *Full House* takes place immediately after the death of Pamela Tanner, who passed away as the victim of a tragic drunk-driving incident. Pamela was survived by her husband (Danny), her daughters (Michelle, Stephanie, and DJ), and her brother (Jesse).

Obviously this was an intensely traumatic event, so it made complete sense for the family to circle the wagons in the aftermath of her death. This is why Jesse, a young and handsome bachelor with rock-star aspirations, put his life on hold to move in with Danny and the girls. He's family after all, and again and again *Full House* would go to significant narrative lengths to emphasize how important family is.

Which is why I could never make any sense out of why Joey *also* moved in. After all, Joey's involvement violated this delicate veil of separation because he wasn't family. In show canon, he's described as Danny's lifelong best friend who moves in with Danny to help raise the girls. I can buy that explanation if the arrangement is temporary. But forever? Forever ever? No, forever seems relegated to the territory of family only.

Which is why Joey's perpetual presence confused me. How can he exist within the natural order of things as set out by the show when he's just a friend? How easy would it have been to have just made him Danny's brother? Being Danny's biological brother would have simplified the arrangement. And since they don't look anything alike, an adoptive brother would have been fine too.

Even more, I know stand-up comedy isn't exactly a dependable gig, but we're supposed to believe that Joey subverted his professional, social, and romantic lives just to be part of a triumvirate of men raising girls? Fishy, right?

Think of when DJ is eighteen, Stephanie is thirteen, and

Michelle is in the late stages of childhood. That's a lot of hormones and emotions to endure for a guy with no biological obligation to stay.

I mean, Joey was an unattached dude. He never woke up and thought, *I just want to go to Costa Rica for a few weeks and see what happens?* Best I can tell, one day he's in his late twenties and then the next day, *boom*, he lives in his best friend's basement and has three surrogate daughters? That's asking a lot for anyone, even a lifelong best friend.

Unless.

Unless you reconsider his motivation.

What if Joey isn't motivated by his friendship to Danny as much as he is by his familial connection to the girls? Stay with me.

Let's talk genetics for a second. As we know, Danny Tanner is a brown-haired man. Pamela Tanner, as best as we can tell, was also brown-haired, which is strange when you think of how DJ, Stephanie, and Michelle are not brown-haired but golden-haired. What are the odds of two brunette people having not just one but three children with blonde hair? I don't know because I'm not smart like that, but I emailed someone who was, and this was the response:

"Please don't bother me anymore with these weird hypotheticals."

Tough, but fair. So I emailed someone else and kept Joey Gladstone's name out of it, and this was the response:

"Very small percentage of likelihood."

So where did those girls get that blonde hair? Let's consider the facts as we know them.

1. A single, competent, attractive man spends the prime of his life voluntarily living in a basement so that he can

operate in some vaguely paternal role for his friend's allegedly biological daughters.

2. This man has golden-blond hair, and he's the only other person in the house, besides the very blonde daughters, with such a fair and beautiful mane.[1]

3. In the years after Pamela's death, Danny showcased very little game and no competency as a romantic catch. He rarely exhibited any sense of humor and seemed more interested in cleanliness and order than he did in spontaneity and fun.

4. It's not a stretch to assume that this rigidity of emotion must have been difficult for the late Pamela Tanner. We aren't privy to her emotional state, but it would be understandable if she'd been discontent in her relationship. She has a husband who is not a lot of fun but does keep her in comfort,[2] so she stays, but all the while as a prisoner to melancholy. Likely all she wants to do is laugh and feel young and free again as a defiant contrast to her current situation. And who do we know as someone who is always orbiting her situation and overqualified in the art of making people laugh? I'm not saying infidelity is right, but in this circumstance I can see how it happened.

5. And since we're here, it feels wrong to not acknowledge the elephant in the room: the girls aren't the only blond children in the home. Don't forget Alex and Nicky. Genetically speaking, Jesse's black hair and Aunt Becky's brown hair make the blondeness of their twins a suspicious outlier.

---

1. I'm not ignoring Comet the golden retriever.
2. *Hamilton* reference.

In closing, while the story of *Full House* wants us to believe one thing, genetics reveals a house full of something other than what we thought we knew. Whatever happened to predictability, indeed.

TWENTY-TWO

CHANGE WILL DO YOU GOOD

When I was too young to remember, my family moved from Athens, Georgia, to Cleveland, Tennessee, for my dad's work. He and my mom had grown up in Cleveland, but his work had led us around the Southeast before our family eventually landed back where my parents had spent most of their lives. And once we'd resettled, my parents dutifully sought out a church that would fit our young family.

Ultimately, after physically landing in Cleveland, we spiritually landed at Westwood Baptist Church, where I would experience the most spiritually formative moments of my life, both good and bad.

Imagine me as Bob Ross for a moment and allow me to paint you a picture of Westwood Baptist Church. Maybe you went to a church just like it, or maybe you've never been to church, but I believe in the value of communicating the texture of places that make us who we are.

I can't definitively say that Westwood was the quintessential small Southern Baptist church in the eighties and nineties, but it felt like it. So I'll report that feeling as fact, and we can move on. Even today, when I think about the construct of church as a physical place, the steeple from Westwood still comes to mind, as does the garish orange carpet outfitting the floor and pews in the sanctuary. It felt huge in the way that all buildings do when you are a child, and, conversely, it looks tiny anytime I drive by it in an indulgent fit of nostalgic passion.

I said earlier that Westwood was the setting of my most significantly formative spiritual moments, and this is true. But it is also an understatement. For many years Westwood Baptist was the only passageway for my heart to consider who God was and what he wanted with my life.

After ten years, my parents left for a church across town that featured a pastor whose sermon repertoire was a bit more diversified. At Westwood, Pastor Bell banged the drum of salvation loudly, consistently, and vividly. As a child, the complexity of salvation and eternity never failed to captivate me (both traumatically and hopefully), but I can understand how my parents were the dead horses beaten into the afterlife by those sermons.

My sister and I remained at Westwood, which worked because Cleveland was a small enough town where my parents could drop us off and still make it to their church in time. This was unconventional, but Westwood had a grip on my sister and me spiritually and socially, so it would take something severe and significant for me to leave.

This is the story of that significant severeness.

On New Year's Day 1993, my family gathered with other Westwood families to celebrate the new year, but mainly to watch college football. We were at the home of my friend James, and the plan for the entire event was the consistent mantra of all Baptist get-togethers: *Food, Fellowship, and Fun.*[1] For ten-year-old me, this sounded great, because I loved all those things. However, somewhat complicating this plan was the presence of James's older brother, Ben, and Ben's friend, Brad.[2]

I say "complicating" because Ben and Brad had the same ominous social presence that any older kids have over younger ones. To younger kids, older kids are always Threat Level Midnight. They are like fireworks, scorpions, or David Blaine—very cool to observe but terrifying to behold up close. There was fascination, obviously, but also a distinct sense of intimidation.

But for most of the day, everything was pretty chill. James and I watched some football, played some football, and indiscriminately tasted every dessert on the food table, all while hanging out with some of the other kids at the party. It was truly majestic.

However, unbeknownst to me, Ben and Brad had been lying in wait like a booby trap.[3]

In retrospect, I don't know if I had always been in their crosshairs or if it was a wrong place / wrong time situation. Regardless, I had unknowingly wandered into their diabolical designs.

Here's how it went down: James and I were taking turns innocently shooting Nerf darts at a bull's-eye target on the living

---

1. Also *Football*. It's not church-sanctioned, but in the South, football is the Frankie Jonas of the other *F*'s—not prioritized but definitely in the same family.
2. I'm going to act like these aren't their real names, but they for sure are their real names.
3. Has the phrase *booby trap* always bothered you like it does me? I looked up its etymology, and *booby* means a "stupid person / slow bird" but, like, that word has evolved a bit, you know? What I'm saying is that, on a tiny level, the need to reconsider this word basically proves the premise of this book.

room wall. One of us would go to the wall, stand on a chair, and unstick all the darts to return them for more firing.

When my turn came to retrieve the darts, Ben and Brad seized the opportunity to shank me. Not in a prison sense of stabbing me with a crudely sharpened tool, but in the pulling-pants-down way. Which, to a fifth grader, feels like the emotional equivalent of, if not worse than, getting stabbed with a crudely sharpened toothbrush.

But as embarrassing as it was, getting shanked wasn't a social extinction–level event. A majority of kids probably endure some version of a shanking at least once in their childhoods.[4]

Is that what I'm communicating here, just a fleeting and mild embarrassment that was quickly forgotten? Let me add some ingredients of calamity to this humiliation layer cake.

For one, we weren't the only people in the room. Remember, it was the living room and this was a party, so there were a lot of eyewitnesses to my shanking. Specifically, the Habermas girls, daughters of the minister of education at Westwood and good friends of our family. The youngest Habermas, Missy, went to school with me, and we were friends the way boy and girl fifth-grade students normally were in that time, because she was very fast and was a classroom roster asset to have come Field Day.

The middlest Habermas, Tracey, was my sister's friend, so she was also someone I regularly saw at slumber parties. The oldest daughter, Sarah, was a cool teenager, and I shouldn't have to

---

4. I hear that some people call this *pantsing*, but I don't like that name. It's not mystical enough. I do like the momentary pause of people trying to understand if I was stabbed or if my pants were pulled down. Again, I think we're trying to access the emotional truth of what's happening here, people.

explain that you just don't want to have your pants pulled down in front of cool teenagers.

While this was definitely embarrassing, it still cannot be described as truly traumatic, right? Well, wait, because there's more: this shanking didn't follow the traditional execution of lowering my pants and just exposing my underwear. Sadly, it was an exceptionally heightened shanking, because Brad and Ben had inadvertently also grabbed my underwear along with my pants, leaving the entirety of my private situation fully exposed. That's correct—it was a biscuits-out-of-the-basket situation.

You get what's going on here. I was full-on, waist-down nude in a very full room of people I worshipped God with—while also elevated on a chair. You forgot the chair part, didn't you? That's understandable because I'm unfurling so many elements at you, but I've never forgotten that aspect. It was almost like I had been perfectly set apart in that moment to be properly humiliated.

I recovered quickly and overcorrected by pulling my under-wear and pants back up to basically my armpits before maturely deciding to retreat into James's bedroom. By retreat, I mean I dove under his bed so hard that I was practically trying to will the space there to become a kind of Narnian retreat. Unfortunately, there was no Narnia for me—just the barrier of a bed allowing me silent contemplation on the ruination of my life.

Reprimands were given and apologies were offered, but the damage was done. How could I be concerned with getting a pound of flesh when too much of my flesh had been flashed to all the wrong people? No, I had moved on to figuring out how to create a new life for myself. Siberia had always sounded fun. Maybe I could move there?

My parents were pretty aloof to any overseas relocation talk, but they did allow me to leave Westwood and start going to church with them. Though I'd spent over a decade there learning about God and forming significant relationships that tethered me to the idea of not just a physical church but also a community, I had to leave. Turns out when your entire peer group sees you in Winnie-the-Pooh status, it's just too much to bear (nailed it), and you have to reassess your place of worship.

And while this was my first reconsideration about church, it definitely would not be the last. In some ways, it's a luxury to be denuded in front of your peer group because it forces you to act.[5] Usually though, reconsidering church is more nuanced.

I had to reconsider what church was to me after leaving home for college. Where would I go? What denomination would it be and how frequently would I attend?

As a couple, Ashley and I had to reconsider church in the face of hurtful words or the departures of friends on staff.

But even more deeply, we've had to reconsider the idea that action, involvement, and our presence in a physical church is a substitute for the activity of our faith. At different points, the act of participating in ministry within a church took priority over a deeper, more necessary process of thinking and feeling and, most of all, experiencing our faith.

For many years, just showing up in church was the climactic action of my day-to-day faith. Sometimes there were peripheral experiences, but they were all routed through whatever physical church we were attending. The sacraments, the events, the experiences, the songs, and the sermons, while all good, felt geolocated to a specific address, which meant they didn't feel as rich or vivid

---

5. Look, I'm making a larger point here, but this is idiotic nonsense.

beyond those walls. It was challenging to find and access my faith outside that specific physical space.

If this comes off like I'm disparaging physical churches, I'm definitely not. They are crucial and necessary to people and communities. But sometimes, if I'm not careful, they and the routine they offer can usurp the function of my faith and become a sort of shorthand for devotion. I love this in the same way I love all-inclusive hotels: because it simplifies things.

But as I've come to find out, faith isn't meant to be simplified or consolidated into a physical location; it's supposed to be complicated and messy and sprawling, and my faith was none of that. Mine was this nice and tidy houseplant that I controlled and loved because of all the control I exerted over it. As much as this is an impulse, it's a disquieting one that persists no matter how dedicated I am to the fiefdom I've made for myself.

In an effort to quell this impulse, I've learned that I can tweak where I worship, what sermons I hear, and what music I sing, but if a deeper change is required, no physical structure will assuage that compulsion. I have to more deeply reconsider my own heart and self-critique what it is I am expecting someone else to fix.

Which, frankly, sucks. It's an uncomfortable experience to spiritually disrobe yourself, but it's to get to something real—it's something you have to do. Even more—and I can say this as a veteran of sorts—it's an action you can't expect anyone else to do, even if you do know a Brad or Ben with a penchant for mischief.

As a postscript, Brad was instrumental in two important events in my life long after the shanking incident: (1) he was my tour guide around Samford University when I was thinking of attending, and he graciously looked after me as a naïve college freshman; and (2) we ran into each other at Dollywood once, and he revealed that he had seen Dolly Parton herself on park grounds, which allowed me and my family to behold the great Dolly live and in person. So I'd say he more than redeemed himself.

TWENTY-THREE

IN THE BEGINNING

It was 2009. I was in bed trying to sleep, but I couldn't because of this book I was reading. Normally, books are like melatonin to me. Ever since I'd learned to read, reading before bed was how I always finished off my day and sent myself off to sleep, but not that night. I couldn't sleep because I was so mad, and it was all Rachel Held Evans's fault.

I had been reading her book *Evolving in Monkey Town*,[1] and the contents made me physically angry. My heart was pounding and my ears were getting red, the telltale signs that my blood pressure was elevating. I was never going to sleep now, and it was all because of Rachel and her progressive ideas.

The biggest offense I'd encountered was her casual acceptance and discussion of evolution as a scientific fact. I cannot even begin to tell you how much of a no-no this was in the South. We rarely ever used the e-word unless it was in reference to the evolution of an SEC offense, and even then, it was whispered

---

1. Since retitled and rereleased as *Faith Unraveled*.

the way the students of Hogwarts whispered "Voldemort," lest we similarly conjure up Charles Darwin or the paleontological remains of a Homo erectus.

More specifically, the way she was talking about evolution was very much perturbing me. Her words were almost audacious in their clarity, and it was jarring to read someone make such a compelling case for something I would never, ever agree with. Which is why I was so mad at Rachel; her book engaged me in a way I didn't expect, and intellectually I couldn't help but consider and respect how she was doing it.

Have you ever been mad at someone, but after a quick logistical audit, you can't identify one single thing they did wrong?[2] That was me with Rachel's book, and this feeling was the primary engine behind my anger.

The first time I heard about evolution was in ninth grade. I was at a new school with teachers I didn't know and just a small handful of friends[3] I'd managed to cobble together. The class was world history with Mr. Burgner, a bearded, burly, no-nonsense teacher.

Some teachers initiate banter with their students, some don't mind its spontaneous appearance, and others are a black hole in which banter goes to spaghettify. Mr. Burgner was the latter. He was an amazing teacher, but this was definitely not a *Dead Poets Society* situation. His lectures were an A+B conversation with him being both letters, and he wanted our commentary to "C him never."

On the day in question, he began a lecture about the fossils of a hominin named "Lucy." Mr. Burgner explained how she was discovered and the implications of what that meant in the larger

---

2. If you are married, you definitely should have said yes to this.
3. In my relational parlance, "handful" equates to two.

tapestry of humanity's steady evolution toward becoming Homo sapiens. In Mr. Burgner's mind, he was setting the foundation for understanding how our species exploded forth and throughout the world (something we would be tested on). But by setting his foundation in place, he was ruining mine.

Here I was, a young Southern Baptist, and Mr. Burgner wasn't just daring to talk about evolution; he was presenting it as the only possibility. Not only that, but I would also be tested on my absorption of this knowledge?

My faith felt waylaid, and I was flabbergasted. Clearly this was the persecution so many people had warned me about,[4] so I was spurred to action. It's important to clarify that young Southern Baptists in the eighties and nineties were raised to anticipate altercations around the basis of our faith, and in retrospect, we were conditioned to misinterpret these altercations as persecutions. Accordingly, Mr. Burgner trying to teach his syllabus was akin to what Paul endured at the hands of the Romans.

Emboldened by this "persecution," my friend Ricky and I began to "debate" him in class. Think about that for a second, because I don't think you are zeroing in on the absurdity of this situation:

- two fourteen-year-old bozos debating a professional educator
- in his own class
- about a topic he'd taught for over twenty years
- and, conversely, one with which we'd been familiar for fifteen minutes

---

4. LOL.

If we could bottle just a fraction of the essential arrogance of teenage boys, there would be no more need for fossil fuels. Also, thoughts and prayers out there to all the high school science teachers who ever lived and taught in the Bible Belt. You all are the real MVPs.

It didn't matter to Ricky and me that we were two fourteen-year-old idiots with little world history knowledge and exactly zero scientific training about evolution. We were fueled by something more powerful than just knowledge: the anger at what we didn't understand.

I was taught that creation happened in six literal days, and on the seventh God rested, which is why we have Sunday. And for most of my life, this worked pretty well. The creation story was a component of my faith, but it wasn't the through line that connected me most immediately to Jesus, the epicenter of my faith. So I just kept ascribing to the veracity of the Genesis account because . . . why not? And what else would be the answer? This subtextual tension was rooted in my belief for most of my life.

But then came the dinosaur issue, which I wrote about in *The Wondering Years*. There I was, a human adult person in his thirties, suddenly trying to reconcile the dinosaur timeline, and honestly? I'm surprised it took so long. I've long been captivated by science, and the mathematical issue of a six-thousand-year-old Earth and a sixty-five-million-year-old crater impact from the meteor that killed the dinosaurs presents a pretty problematic math equation.

And even though my MO on issues like this, particularly

in matters of faith, was to approach them in a black-and-white manner, this was the first instance when I realized that both the Bible and the scientific timeline of the dinosaurs could be true— and even more, that it was necessary for me to not just have the capacity to hold seemingly conflicting truths but also to attempt to reconcile them.

I want to be clear: I don't mean "necessary" in a prosecutorial sense but in the sense of needing to achieve harmony with how God made me and how I synchronized my beliefs about the world with my understanding of it.

I obviously believed in God and the Bible, but I also trusted science. Somehow this arrangement was turning into the Capulets versus the Montagues, with me as Romeo and Juliet. I wanted to secretly intertwine these two things but never felt like I could. I felt pushed to choose a side in the fair Verona of my heart.

To me, science always seemed collaborative with God. It was trustworthy in that the only thing it pursued was the confirmation of truth—and wasn't truth God's whole thing? But for some reason, Christians always looked at science with a scowl, as though science had the potential to usurp God. But if God was the author of all things, science would only further reveal this. And while that might mean we have to adapt our understanding of God and the cosmos, that doesn't mean that he himself is in danger. You know, because he's, like, God.

But sometimes clinging to our understanding of God is the god we worship, and we prefer that iteration over the real one. And I understand that impulse! Assuredness is much more comfortable than the idea that you might have to periodically recalibrate your perception of God/existence/eternity.

But to me, having to recalibrate and reconsider isn't indicative of a problem; it's indicative of growing our understanding of the divine as we grow to understand ourselves and the world around us.

Otherwise, I'm asked to believe the idea that after a six-week study series on whatever biblical topic, I can pretty much have everything figured out. To me, that mind-set takes entirely more faith than I could ever muster.

It's important to examine our why when it comes to clinging to specific beliefs. Is it because we believe in them so fully and completely that anything less would seem disrespectful? Or is it because we prize the stability of our beliefs above all else, even more than their content?

For example, it's funny how once you feel like you have a bead on who God is, you can feel the need to hold on to that supposition for dear life, no matter what that belief entails or suggests. Why do we do this? Is it because we're defending the sacred honor of God? Maybe (but probably not). Or is it because this behavior allows us to manipulate how we understand God? Or better yet, because it lets us manipulate who, to us, God actually is?

Something I can really break my brain contemplating is the literal body of God. Broadly, we understand that we don't have any kind of authentic representation of God. It's not like there's footage of God loping through the forest, a la Bigfoot. The construction of God's physicality is largely just an exercise we do because we have to have *something*. We know that we are created in God's image, which means that God has to kind of resemble us, right? He can't look like an octopus or anteater because, image-wise, that wouldn't track even just a little.

Many of us have settled on an image of God as an Old Guy with a White Beard because, traditionally, old, white-bearded men connote a certain prestige of age and wisdom. But we really don't know. God could just as easily look like the Gerber baby. Or Chunk from *The Goonies* or Denzel Washington in *Remember the Titans*. Do I really think that is possible? No, but these are understandable manifestations that help us get a more comfortable foothold into the larger idea of who God is.

But even that effort itself is a fool's errand. To suppose that we can nail down any aspect of the galvanizing force of existence beyond what has already been communicated is just incorrect. Which gets me back to the brain-breaking part. Trying to put an appearance on God is as useless as trying to put a backstory on God. It's just not going to happen. We can assume that God is an old guy with a long beard and an affinity for long, flowing white gowns, but all of those suppositions are entirely about us, not him.

Back to evolution. As it was explained to me, evolution was an attack on Christianity because it removed the need for God. If God didn't make Adam and Eve and insert them into the garden of Eden, then humanity didn't have a creator. If we created ourselves, then we probably also created God.

But the removal of that belief about evolution being an attack brought me into a deeper confidence about the essence of God. Let me explain.

The neatness of God's intersection into our lives never felt right to me. This is God, after all, but yet we're constantly contextualizing him like he's Tom Cruise from the *Mission: Impossible* movies—larger than life, sure, but almost hilariously digestible. In other words, we create this situation that unless God can make sense to us, he can't be God. Ergo, we try to depict and qualify him in a way that satisfies this human need while also maintaining his divine God-ness.

But the neater and more quantifiable God became, the less I understood him. I made him into an old man in a white cloak in the sky because that's how my mind needed to process it, but that couldn't be God, right?[5]

I even wondered about the gendered version of God as a man. I know we're made in his image, but was that literal? Like with a five-o'clock shadow and hairy ears?

Strangely, the more I wrestle with this, the more the Old Testament has helped me. I know the Old Testament has typically been the place where God makes less sense, but I find the rawness of the language and the experiences he's depicted in as comfortingly confusing. The characterization of God as a divine flame or a cloud of glory actually makes more sense to me now. It might be weird, but I prefer that because it allows me to broaden the lens of how I try to think about God, which was always the seminal difficulty of my faith as a kid.

As a child, when I was trying to build out an understanding of God and the context surrounding him, he was just this divine person with Earth in his purview, but I didn't know anything else. Was he a part of a divine ruling dynasty and we were in his territory? Did God look at us like the Panama City of places he oversaw, or more like New York City? Were we his first creation? His only creation? Were we his punishment?

My childlike articulation of God intensified these questions and funneled my misunderstanding into a particular direction because I was always having to fit him into the preexisting narratives I'd had foisted upon me. But what if I allowed myself to start over and keep only the idea that I believed in a benevolent God

5. Like, why would God wear white? Every time I wear white, I somehow find something with mustard and immediately drop it on my shirt.

who was both present in my existence but far beyond anything I could comprehend?

From there, instead of an old white-bearded guy with a cloak, what if this new idea of God transcended traditional gender?

What if he wasn't an element within the universe, but he was the essential fabric of the universe?

Yes, I was deconstructing the primary framework about God that I'd kept my entire life, but this change was something necessary for me to continue. It wasn't quite adapt or die, but it was a similar kind of evolution.

I never had the pleasure of knowing Rachel Held Evans in real life despite growing up and living just minutes from her.[6] Sadly, she passed away in 2019, but her humanization of challenging Christian convention, asking tough questions, and holding people accountable is a legacy that will live far beyond her brilliant writing.

Back in 2009, though, I was legitimately mad at her because I wasn't ready to understand the cognitive dissonance that she provoked in me. I wanted affirmation and simplicity, but instead I was getting complication, and I had been taught that complication was an enemy of faithfulness. But was it really?

We cling to affirmation and simplicity out of a need for security, but this hurts us because it renders us unable to

---

6. I was once invited into a secret Facebook group that included her, but I think I was added accidentally. This perception was put into sharp relief when a semifamous Christian-adjacent writer threatened to curbstomp me to death over my opinions about *The Walking Dead*.

reconsider. Prioritizing stability is completely understandable, but it comes at the cost of better understanding something through reconsideration.

And I'm not talking just about evolution. We overlook a lot so that we can avoid the complicated process of reconsideration:

- scientifically incorrect ideology
- the necessity of more *Toy Story* movies
- systemic marginalization of disenfranchised groups
- Armie Hammer being a thing
- racist and misogynistic power structures

In a vacuum, I think we all agree that these are things we should change. However, the reconsideration necessary requires not just understanding the underlying truth but also understanding the action needed to precipitate that change. And because of this difficulty, these problematic things persist because the need for change isn't overwhelmingly urgent to enough people.

On a granular level, this is a lot like what happens with our own individual beliefs. Prior to (and even while) reading Rachel's book, my continued policy of opting for affirmation and simplicity over reconsideration, while understandable, ignored a much-needed self-assessment asking me to better understand why I believed what I believed. As much as I didn't like the changes this provoked, it was an evolution my soul absolutely required.

TWENTY-FOUR

THE GOOD PLACE

It's funny: I can't really remember the moment when someone first told me about heaven. I know I was very young, but I feel like that's something I would remember. I suppose it is possible that I never formally learned about heaven as much as I absorbed its reality—and to be fair, it's a vivid reality that we're eager to absorb. But that doesn't mean that understanding it is any easier.

People talked about heaven in a way that made it seem like a divine conclusion or spiritual climax,[1] but in my imagination I envisioned it as something like when Templeton goes to the fair in *Charlotte's Web.*

If you haven't seen the animated version of *Charlotte's Web,* first of all, what are you even doing? And second, why doesn't anyone love you?

Third, Templeton at the fair in *Charlotte's Web* may be my favorite musical number of all time, and that's saying something because you've seen my many *Hamilton* references. It's mostly

---

1. Trust me, I don't love this phrasing either, but you get it.

my favorite because the song Templeton sings, "A Veritable Smorgasbord," is the ultimate anthem for people who love food. Some people love food like they love air; others love food only in relationship to their ability to deny it; and some love the comfort and deliciousness that food represents. I'm in that last category, as is Templeton, a literal rat who wants to get his eat on when he's suddenly given the opportunity to go to the Mecca of delicious foods: a county fair.

I can't stress enough the orgiastic collision of unhealthy foods with your waistline that happens at a county fair. Anything that can be fried, kettled, or barbecued is, and all of it is uniformly delicious. So Templeton is definitely not throwing away his shot,[2] and he's certainly not underplaying the immensity of this occasion. He has reached his reward in gluttonous heaven.

There's a terrifyingly accurate analogy between Templeton and me when it comes to heaven. The way Templeton's ticket to the fair would be punched involved him helping Charlotte with errands related to Wilbur. In other words, Templeton wasn't going out of the goodness of his heart as much as he 100 percent wanted to be let loose among the discarded corn dogs and donuts.

Similarly, early in my attempt to understand heaven, the biggest draw to me was eternally experiencing endless chicken nuggets while floating in a vast and properly cooled lazy river during breaks from playing with velociraptors. I know that's weird and strangely specific, but that's what sounded like paradise to me as a kid.

The idea of capitalizing on an opportunity to get to a good place also resonated with me. For most of my life, I don't know

---

2. *Hamilton* reference.

that I could accurately separate my motivations for wanting to go to heaven.

a. Was it because heaven was a very cool place?
b. Was it because it wasn't hell?
c. Was it because God and Jesus were there, and that's where I should also want to be?

If this question came up in Sunday school, I would dutifully raise my hand for option C. But nothing could be further from the actual truth. In reality, most of my motivation for heavenly ascendance has been aligned with reasons A and B.

I'll be completely transparent and vulnerable with you here. A lot of authors will write in a language that is more a collection of Jesus bingo phrases than a reflection of authentic feelings, especially when it comes to heaven. I've read people who refer to their fixation on heavenly reward and their eagerness to praise God and Jesus in heaven for eternity, but that has decidedly not been my vibe because I've never really understood heaven as anything beyond an ethereal reward. Believe me, I'm not saying this with pride; rather, I'm admitting that for me to give myself over to something, I demand understanding.

On its own, that sentiment sounds noble and laudable, but it's really about control. I try to control my belief through understanding it. That way I feel more comfortable giving myself over to it. But faith doesn't really work that way. Like, *at all*.

Now, I think there's room for grace here. It's imperative for us to seek out a better understanding and not rely on ignorance and obliviousness as a sort of avatar for devoutness. But there comes a point when you just can't achieve complete understanding of everything. You reach the edge of your own understanding, and you have to give yourself over to not just the mystery of it all but the insecurity of placing your trust in something else.

This is difficult for me in general but especially when it came to trying to understand what heaven is really like. You can understand how I might have grappled with the realities of the hereafter given the traditional tent-pole elements of the way heaven was marketed to me:

1. **Mansions:** Love 'em. Ever since I watched *DuckTales*, I've wanted a mansion. But aren't too many mansions bad for the real estate economy? Also, a mansion looks like a ton of house to clean by yourself. What if I really just want one of those super-nice-looking tiny houses that looks like something the super wealthy, one-percenter Keebler Elves lived in?

2. **Jewels:** This one was tough because I'm not a precious stones kind of guy. You probably knew that if you looked at my author photo, but in case you didn't, please now know that about me. Plus, does the presence of jewels and crowns of jewels mean there's currency in heaven? I've barely mastered our own currency and things like interest rates here on earth, so this is not ideal for me.

3. **Streets of gold:** Why do we need streets when we can fly? We can fly, can't we? Please tell me we can fly. What even *is* heaven if we can't fly?

4. **Eternal worship:** So we're potentially worshipping forever? Like forever-ever in a praise-and-worship sense? I love "Shout to the Lord" as much as the next guy, but can we finesse this whole thing into a silently-and-to-myself kind of praise and worship?

5. **People you love:** This one was never properly clarified for me, because I was taught that we will be physically with the people we love, *or* we will just be able to recognize them but without the earthly relationships that connected us to them. Which always made me incredibly sad. Why wouldn't I be able to experience heaven with the people I loved on earth just as I experienced life with them? I get that not everyone's idea of paradise is being with their earthly family, but it is mine, so what's the legality of this kind of thing in heaven?

It's difficult to reconsider heaven because I barely know anything about it. It has the same mystique as your ultimate destination while you're on an incredibly long car ride: more "Are we there yet?" than "What will happen once we are there?" I think we like to trick ourselves into believing we know much more than we do. To be sure, there are biblical passages we can point to that potentially provide an outline of heaven, but the more I consider what I believe, the less I think I know.

The famous movie director J. J. Abrams is known for his mystery-box theory, which he incorporates into most of his movies. The essential idea of the mystery box is something that presents a mystery and then preserves that mysteriousness as a way of intensifying its effect. The idea is that once you reveal the specificities of a mystery, it immediately becomes less compelling because you can define and understand it.

I often wonder about this idea in relation to heaven. Maybe the mystery and our lack of knowledge surrounding it intentionally subverts our reactions to and motivations for that knowledge. If heaven really is all the chicken nuggets, lazy rivers, and velociraptors I wanted, and I could verify that, how would that affect my behavior here and now? Conversely, if heaven isn't an actual place but instead a state of mind, would that change my motivations for being there?

In other words (to hijack an improper but already extended metaphor), what if heaven isn't a literal eternity where Templeton gets to be at a fair with all kinds of delicious food? What if instead it is a state of consciousness that gives the same effect?

What I think about heaven now is very different from what I'd always believed, not only in content but in how definitive I am about the particulars. My biggest reconsideration is about feeling confident about how much I do not know. And while I'll never find the comfort of tangible understanding, I'm finding a lot of reassurance in being forced to give myself over to the mystery of it all.

TWENTY-FIVE

THE GOD CARD

Let's take a brief pause from our reconsidering sojourn so that we might do a proper sideswipe on the concept known as the "God Card." For the purposes of this chapter, I'm going to talk about it through the prism of my faith, but this is a concept that transcends religion. The premise of the God Card is the same, whether you believe in the Jesus, Buddha, or Beyoncé.

In practice, the God Card is a device used by people to validate their actions or decisions. A frequent verbal manifestation of the God Card is, "I've been led/called to do [insert action]." Usually it's in reference to someone wanting to become a missionary or start a ministry for a marginalized portion of society. Great things, right?

However, complications arise when people begin to ascribe the God Card to actions and decisions that may not be completely God-divined. Therein lies the problem/brilliance of its use.

First, it communicates that you are very much about that God life. Second, it indicates that whatever decision you've made, God himself has stamped his divine and supernatural approval upon it, so good luck changing the outcome. Because of this almost opulent vagueness, you can't fact-check a person's use of the God Card.

Your friend Gary may have told you that God has called him to take out a small home equity loan so that he can turn his basement into a deluxe man cave, but as much as that smells like a lie, it's not like you can cross-check his assertion with God.

EXT. OUTSIDE A STARBUCKS—AFTERNOON

God exits Starbucks holding a grande iced coffee and lemon loaf. You approach him like a frenzied journalist trying to crack open a huge story.

YOU

God! God, quick question. Gary said you told him to dip into his home equity so that he can turn his basement into a man cave. Care to comment?

GOD

As always, I'm directing all comments to my publicist. But off the record?

YOU

(lowers voice to a whisper) Of course.

GOD

A man cave, really? Gross. What is
this, an HGTV episode from 2009?

Obviously, playing the God Card is a pretty powerful move because it functions as a sort of spiritual checkmate. Who can argue with something God has initiated?

This gets complicated because I honestly do believe that God still moves in our hearts and minds, so sometimes playing the God Card is authentic and real. But I want to urge all of us to reconsider the frequency with which we are deftly deploying the God Card, and when I say "deftly" I am totally being sarcastic. If only there were a sarcastic font, that would have been a perfect time to use it.[1]

So let's dive into the different ways we misuse the God Card:

1. **To justify something completely bananas.** This is like the man cave example, or, if you want me to escalate the banananess, it can be something like, "My boyfriend and I want to get pregnant so we can be on MTV's *16 and Pregnant* because it's a great platform from which to share the gospel."

2. **To camouflage ambition.** Especially in Christian circles, ambition can be a funny thing. The God Card is a good counterbalance, as it allows for ambition to be properly presented through a religious lens: "I've been called to

---

1. Seriously, how do we not have a sarcastic font yet? I can have an emoji unicorn face shriek via text but no sarcastic font? Tim Cook, let's reconsider our priorities, k?

take a new job that will triple my salary and has one of those community kitchens where there are snack drawers with a delicious array of foods that I'm allowed to eat whenever I want." God might have called you there, or you just like the idea of more money and more snacks. No shame in that.

3. **To qualify something you don't want to or can't explain.** This version of the God Card is used as an emotional barrier to derail further inquiry into your motivation: "I can't take part in our family pictures where we're all wearing denim because I'm in a season of God leading me away from all denim fabrics." You could explain that it's really because you don't look good in denim, but you know how vain that sounds to say out loud, so why not just play the God Card?

As much as the idea of the God Card can frustrate me, I know that it exists because God exists, and sometimes he will stir your heart and soul in a way that you can't properly articulate. He'll do it so you know that there's something you just have to do—even if it's beyond explanation or justification.

But using it as much as we do or in circumstances when it doesn't reflect the truth can lead us to be suspicious of *any* use and give us a "The Person Who Cried God Card" feeling.

I know all this from experience. It's easier to say that you are "being led" or "being called" than to explain the personal nuances of taking a different job or moving away. I have misleveraged the God Card myself—not to be dishonest, because I did believe God was moving in my heart and in Ashley's about moving from Tennessee to Birmingham. But by using it, I was allowed to defer to that in lieu of explaining to those closest to me why we were leaving. I avoided the explanation because I have an allergic reaction to feelings and emotions (particularly messy ones), but also because it was really, really difficult for me to try to explain something that was so evident and true in my soul.

Bottom line: I think the use of the God Card is most often about our eagerness to initiate a confluence between God's plan and our own. In the best situations, those things should be in harmony, but too often our decisions are heavily loaded toward our own designs, thus the increasing hollowness of invoking God's stamp of approval. God may really, really want you to build that man cave, Gary, but think long and hard before you go around advertising that assumption.

TWENTY-SIX

THE BAD PLACE

"It's got good bones, this house," literally everyone told me both before and after we finalized the purchase for our house in Birmingham. And it does. It was built in the eighties, and the original owner painstakingly cared for it, which is a good thing until you realize that "cared for it" is shorthand for "not street legal" wiring and stylistic choices that were comprehensively brown and brazenly overconfident.

Nevertheless, the underlying appeal of our house is the good bonedness of it, which stands in contrast to Ashley's and my usual MO of buying homes. Prior to moving to Birmingham, all our homes were purchased directly from the builders just after they finished construction. We liked the newness and the warranties that a newly built house comes with, and we were (and are) convinced that we are not emotionally built for the elongated process of building. We own our impatience and inexperience with contractors and construction, so newly built houses had been a perfect compromise, the newness of the home being a hedged bet against the surprise of urgent and expensive issues to fix.

Conversely, older homes come with the always looming threat of repairs. And the Birmingham house was no different. The rebellion began almost immediately, and it promised to be complicated and expensive. There were leaks and electrical shorts. Some appliances would hiccup while others would unceremoniously die. Ultimately the most expensive and frustrating element was the air conditioner. It was very moody about when it wanted to cool our home, which is not ideal when it's summer in the South. After a lot of dollars spent on diagnosing the issue, the consensus was that our air conditioner was "finicky." I don't know if you know this, but if you ask your home warranty company to replace your air conditioner because it's "finicky," they usually just laugh before hanging up.

So I accepted my new role as Air Conditioner Whisperer. The issues I encounter are never severe enough to call someone out to deal with it, but they do require a certain amount of trial and error.

Usually something will trip our air conditioner's circuit, which requires me to reset it—but not just from the breaker box in our garage. Sadly, I have to descend deep into the dark and angry bowels of our crawl space to flip a switch there as well.

As a policy, I try to avoid crawl spaces as much as possible, because that's where critters, varmints, and serial killers hang out, and I don't want to encounter any of those, probably in that order. But in Alabama summers, to ensure proper cooling, you don't have the luxury of avoiding these things.

The most recent time I had to reset the air conditioner, I opened the door of the crawl space and was greeted by the corpse of a big, bloated black snake at the entrance. I immediately shut the door and wondered if it was too early to begin drinking.

Similar to putting off the deeper systemic issues troubling our air conditioner, I've put off reconsidering hell for a really long time. This is not to be confused with a general awareness of hell. I've been aware of hell my entire life in the same way that I've been aware of all the major neon-sign elements of Christianity. But I've always been more acquainted with the mythicality of hell than with its place in eternity and how I reconcile it within my faith.

To be sure, some of my holding hell at arm's length is because to think deeply about hell is to contemplate the grotesque and horrific, and I don't know about you, but I like to keep my consideration lighter and fluffier.

But I've mostly avoided hell because it's just never been something for me to consider intersecting with. There are no Venn diagrams with me and hell overlapping. It's like how I feel about equestrianism: I'm vaguely aware of what it means to be an equestrian, but that's pretty much it. I don't speak horse, I have trust issues when it comes to large animals, and the clothing required of participants is very much at odds with my body type. For these reasons and more, I avoid learning too much about equestrianism because that knowledge will just be wasted space.

Add to this the reality that I've requested the gift of salvation somewhere around fourteen thousand times[1] throughout my life, leading me to assume that, while I may be fixated on salvation to the point of unhealthiness, ending up in hell is not something I will have to contend with. Also, culturally, I've always resided within the evangelical Christian community, so even as I've been worried for my own salvation, it's sort of a controlled worry. In

---

1. And been instrumental in leading over ten thousand dogs to Christ. (This is a reference to my first book, *The Wondering Years*, and will make absolutely no sense unless you've read it.)

this sense, it feels a lot like taking a spelling test. With most words, I can get close enough to where my effort is a probably pretty close approximation of the answer I'm pursuing. Similarly, as an evangelical, I find that while there is a preoccupation with hell, that preoccupation is also subconsciously soothing.

So you can understand why contemplating hell rarely makes it on my weekly to-do list. But in recent months I've tried to intentionally think about it more, not because I want to but because it seems like the parts of your faith that are the hardest to look at are often the spaces where you need to shine a light the most.

After a long pause outside the crawl space, during which I googled the local availability of a full-body suit of medieval armor and the inherent necessity of air conditioning in July in Alabama, I pep-talked myself into dragging out the very large and very dead black snake with a rake. I managed this despite half expecting it to have been playing dead the entire time for the express purpose of sneak-attacking me and biting me in the face. It never did, though, and I triple garbage-bagged it and stuffed it into our trash can before returning to the foot of our crawl space.

Though the snake was gone, my fear was still actively present, and not without good reason. In analyzing the snake situation, I had two options of belief:

1. This was the Neil Armstrong of snakes and, as such, the first to ever set foot (belly?) onto the real estate of my crawl space.

2. This was just one snake in a long line of other black snakes that regularly traversed my crawl space.[2]

During this analysis, my oldest daughter came outside to check on my progress. From her point of view, it had been thirty minutes since I'd disappeared to fix the air conditioning, and yet it still wasn't on.

SIDDA GRAY

Daddy, why isn't the air on yet?

KNOX

I ran into a complication.

SIDDA GRAY

Are you scared to go in?

KNOX

That's ridiculous. Of course not.
Don't be ridiculous.

SIDDA GRAY

Because I would be scared. It's so dark
in there. I bet animals live in there,
like tons of them. Creepy ones too.

---

2. There was a third rail of belief that I wouldn't allow myself to entertain, which involved the occasion of this snake's death. Why had it occurred? Was it through natural causes or at the hands (fangs?) of another, bigger, and nastier snake?

KNOX

Can we not with the creepiness of the
crawl space?

SIDDA GRAY

Is that why you haven't gone in yet?

KNOX

No, I'm just being thorough.

SIDDA GRAY

What does *thorough* mean? Does it mean
something where you take forever?

KNOX

It means to be very careful and steady.

SIDDA GRAY

So when you go to the bathroom and
stay in there forever, are you being
thorough?

KNOX

Yes, but only because I'm reading.

SIDDA GRAY

Why do you read when you go to the
bathroom? That's gross.

KNOX

Shouldn't you be helping your mom with
something?

SIDDA GRAY

She sent me out here to check on you. She
said you were probably scared to go in.
I'll tell her you are being thorough,
like when you go the bathroom.

The beautiful thing about kids is their often-unadulterated curiosity with the world. Honestly, I don't even know if *curiosity* is the right word. They just have an impulse to populate their intellectual landscape with understanding. I've found that my kids' curiosity (for lack of a better word) can be an engine kick-starting my own desire to understand things, in part because they often ask me to explain things to them, but also because they remind me that I take my own understanding for granted.

For example, prior to kindergarten, my son required two more shots so that he would be properly vaccinated. As good parents we wanted to mentally prepare him for what was going to happen at the pediatrician,[3] so we told him that he would be getting two shots. Naturally, he freaked out and lamented this reality for the entirety of the day in advance of his appointment because

---

3. With our other two children, we amended this approach to more of a "Surprise! You're getting a shot in three, two, one . . ." strategy.

he "didn't want to get shots," which I understood, because who doesn't get a little freaked out by the thought of needles?

When the time came, he took his injections pretty impressively, but even after he was done, he still cried fearfully. When I asked him why, he replied that he just wanted the nurse to bring the gun in and get it over with.

I was confused for a moment until I realized that he interpreted "shots" as "gunshots," thus his dread. This beautiful son of mine had followed me to the doctor, where he assumed I was going to allow him to be shot with a gun not once, but twice. It broke my heart. Truly. His innocence, his trust, my unintentional frivolousness with language, and the horror he must have felt for those few hours in the lead-up to his shots really messed with me.

It was enough to make me want to be much more intentional in how casual I was with words and ideas that were new to our kids. But even more, it made me wonder, what else had I blindsided them with as poorly explained realities of the world?

This coincided with the beginning of truly reconsidering for the first time what I believed about hell.

When I became a father, all the biblical passages about and allusions to God as a father suddenly seemed so much more vivid to me. I was aware of the purpose of this language before becoming a dad, but it crystallized emphatically after my kids were born. The richness of the analogy deepened, but along with this deepening came a tension regarding the reality of hell and the perpetuation of hell as an eternal punishment. As much as I knew that the language of God as a father was never meant to be a one-to-one match for my experience as a father, I couldn't help but recoil at the idea of casting one of my kids out of my presence and into torment for eternity. I know God is God and I am not, but the mystery of God seemed small in contrast to a world where this kind of punishment was commensurate with the crime.

The idea of accepting this wild contrast between punishment and crime confused me, as did the realization that we almost fetishize vindication through the punishment of our enemies. In the Christianity I grew up with, there was a certain gleeful vocabulary about how certain people were going to bust hell wide open and burn, and it made me wonder how to reconcile this almost giddy impulse with Jesus' call to love our neighbor.

I don't always love my neighbors as I should. To be frank, I rarely *like* them as I should. But them burning in flames? I definitely do not want that, and especially not for eternity.

This eternity aspect always chewed at me. It was difficult for me to square a generic lifespan of seventy-ish years against the backdrop of eternity. The idea that our fate for eternity depended on the net trickle-down effect of our deeds within a very small window of that eternalness didn't make a ton of sense. I recognized the cleanliness of this arrangement as a clarified vision of how it all worked, but it just felt uniformly extreme.

Extreme in the vastness of seventy years versus eternity.

Extreme in the punishment of eternal torture as a result of temporal denial.

Extreme in how cut-and-dried it was, especially in contrast to how ancient Jews believed that the afterlife was a shadowy underworld where they would encounter their logical conclusion.[4]

This evidentiary presence of an evolving concept of the afterlife would often lead me down the road of wondering about the fluidity of how this finality was applied to people who lived prior

---

4. See verses such as Genesis 37:35.

to Jesus, prior to Abraham, or prior to even monotheism. For something so definitive, like eternally definitive, the specifics of what counted and when seemed awfully difficult to pin down with absolute certainty.

So I did the best thing I knew to do: I read. I read as much as I could, and as varied perspectives as I could, in hopes that I would discover something to help it all make sense.

But even more, I read because so often, reading is where I encountered God. I found him not only in a church or a Sunday school class, and not only the Christian Living section of Barnes & Noble, but through words and ideas in a frantic pursuit of searching for what only God truly knows.

I found three broadly accepted schools of thought related to hell. It should be obvious that I'm not the originator of any of these ideas, nor am I in the top one million trillion of people who should be clarifying them here. But it's my book, and I'll try to present these ideas as cleanly as possible so as to respect the scholarship that painstakingly went into their formation.

Option 1: Hell is a place dedicated to eternal conscious torment.

Option 2: Hell is separation from God, manifested by unbelievers being annihilated from existence as punishment following their judgment.

Option 3: Hell exists alongside the perpetual opportunity for people to be reconciled with God and thus brought out of hell and into God's presence.

Obviously, option 3 stands out as weirdly hopeful, especially in contrast to the first two options. I've never considered hope as a possibility when it comes to thinking about hell, but this option allows for that. However, it also feels like the option most likely to be booed and accused of being "millennial hippie garbage ideology" in most evangelical congregations.

To this point, though, option 3 squares most with what I want reality to be. The idea of verses like 1 Corinthians 15:22 or 2 Peter 3:9 being indicators of an ultimate reconciliation with God is what I hope is true, because honestly, I don't like anything about the traditional way hell has been presented to me. It feels overly harsh, distractingly vindictive, and cobbled together with haphazardness; and most of all, it feels inconsistent with the God I interpret from Scripture.

But just because I want the possibility of hope to exist in tandem with my understanding of hell doesn't mean it does. I cannot deny that it almost feels like an existential requirement for there to be a mechanism of judgment or purification holding us accountable for our failures and evils here on earth. But as to the infiniteness of that accountability, the severity of it, and whether it is morally righteous to include eternal torment or complete and utter annihilation—that's where I get a little lost.

When confronted with this idea of men wanting eternal punishment to not mean permanent punishment, Augustine wrote in *The City of God*, "Plainly it will be so if the conjectures of men are to weigh more than the word of God. But because this is absurd, they who desire to be rid of eternal punishment ought to abstain from arguing against God, and rather, while yet there is opportunity, obey the divine commands."[5]

It's a withering admonishment from a venerated Christian,

---

5. Saint Augustine, *The City of God*, trans. Marcus Dods (Peabody, MA: Hendrickson, 2009), 716.

enough to almost make me feel shamed into stuffing these ideas deep into a mental drawer. Augustine is Augustine, and who even am I? But what if I'm trying toward obedience in the pursuit of better understanding God's intentions and motives?

Ultimately, options of belief aside, to me the question of hell comes down to the question of identifying God's endgame with us. Is it about justice? Punishment? Magnifying his own glory? Or reconciliation?

I'm not here to tell you what that should be or that you are wrong if you don't believe like I do. But I do believe that God is ultimately about reconciliation. I say that admitting that this doesn't give me any larger clarity on who God is and how that belief squares with the validity of hell. If anything, it makes things more complicated. But I mean, we're talking about God, eternity, morality, and the afterlife. Did you think these things were going to be simple?

———

After wasting more than enough time, I moved into the cool darkness of the crawl space, eager to fix the air conditioner. I was well aware of the reality that I'd be down there again, probably very soon. I further wondered about that later point and whether at that appointed time there would be more dead snakes waiting for me. Or worse yet, alive ones.

I thought about saving our money or taking out a loan so that we could replace our unit, but I quickly dismissed that possibility because (1) it's expensive, and (2) secretly, as untalented as I am at fixing things, I like having to be the one to fix this specific issue. A new air conditioner would work and come with a warranty, but in this specific season, there's something weirdly enjoyable about everything I'm having to learn and all the problems I have to address myself.

This house, and the sometimes-problematic elements that come with it, is annoying, to be sure. It's also probably taken years off my life, but the stress is mitigated by our connection to it. We pay for it monthly but also emotionally; the house was the product of a tumultuous and passionate life change for us.

It is a virtual certainty that more expensive surprises will arise and that new elements will require reconsideration and possibly replacement. There may even be a day down the road where we replace the air conditioner, paint the front of the house, and tear up all the floors and finish unfinished rooms. But it's going to be hard to leave this house because of the bones underneath it all. A lot of the house may change, and a lot of it needs to change, but the bones are what will always keep us.

TWENTY-SEVEN

PREACHERS-IN-SNEAKERS

In 2019 an account called PreachersNSneakers emerged on Instagram with the intent to showcase preachers wearing fashionable (and expensive) sneakers. Famous pastors were photographically documented with their stylish footwear, alongside a confirmed retail value of their shoes. As you can imagine, this set off a firestorm of conversation regarding a great many things, but the bulk of the focus centered on the ethical quandry of professional Christians, their acceptance of materialistic culture, and how these professional Christians should or should not spend their money. All very breezy topics to consider, to be sure.

According to later interviews, the creator of the account clarified that he never intended for it to exist as any kind of commentary beyond presenting the sneaker stylings of different Christian ministers. And even though I believe these words, what he originally intended for the account no longer really applies, because PreachersNSneakers has morphed to satisfy a more urgent tension: that of the very bad optics of Christian pastors wearing excessively expensive shoes.

And to be clear, preachers wearing fashionable and expensive footwear isn't the central problem, but it is symptomatic of a deeper ethical inconsistency stylishly represented one Instagram post at a time.

The argument over the content on PreachersNSneakers quickly split into two distinctly different sides: those who believe pastors have a God-given right to spend money however they please and those who recognize the bad optics of pastors repping fashion and shoes onstage that retail well into the quadruple digits.

Both sides are a little right and a little wrong, and I think most people arrive at this realization pretty quickly. But I think the more fascinating reconsideration is why this nuance exists and what is motivating people to feel so strongly on either side. And to do that, I think we need to look more deeply at the intersection of professional Christians with materialism, secular culture, and money.

To be sure, a subconscious element of this issue is a Christianized lament over the slow and steady sprawl of secular culture into Christian culture. Here, that sprawl is manifested by the expensive shoe choices of these pastors, but the sprawl is evident throughout modern Christianity in other ways too: Christian movies, TV, music, and art all borrow heavily from established formats, tropes, and styles within secular culture. So of course a normalized relationship with secular culture makes sense, especially given the questionable quality of certain modern-day Christian media. At times Christian culture suffers from too heavy a focus on commenting upon and reinforcing itself; in this way, it is a bit like a fart giving an interview about its own smell. It can come across as redundant and reductive precisely because it is a closed loop of inspiration and execution. No wonder pastors, in their attempts to be fashionable either for vanity reasons (likely) or self-expression reasons (unlikely but probably the go-to answer), tend toward secular fashion, and double no wonder that other superficially secular elements also trickle into the larger Christian Industrial Complex.

Back when I was a kid, pastors looked like characters from *The Office*. And not cool characters like Jim or Ryan; characters like Toby, Kevin, and Creed. And I loved this dynamic because there was something disarming and graceful about a man who looked like he was always in a twelve-hour window of having a mustard stain on his person. It's either a miracle or proof of God that such a schlub is allowed to speak on the divine's behalf, and it might be both.

Slowly, though, pastors began to evolve their fashion sense. At first they dressed like models in an Old Navy commercial. Later it became the Gap. Now pastors dress like the Chainsmokers. That's a band, but pastors also dress like people who look like they chain-smoke. It's confusing. It's all weird farmer hats, distressed skinny jeans, and tight V-neck shirts I could never pull off even if I were given The Rock's body. It's very disorienting.

Turning this in another direction, this is why Christians flipped out so much in 2019 when Kanye West came out with a gospel album.[1] Christians are so obsessed with cultural

---

1. I'm laughing as I write this because, by the time you read this, literally anything is possible when it comes to Kanye West and his connection to Christianity. He could become a cult leader, the next Billy Graham, an avowed Satanist, or almost any other thing the mind could dream up. Just know that in this moment, I'm writing this pretty close to when white Christians uniformly loved Kanye and he appeared at Joel Osteen's church in a bizarre appearance that also alleged Hollywood mind-control experiments on our children.

affirmation that we very enthusiastically attach ourselves to anyone who pays even the most modest lip service to our faith if they come from a place of secular credibility.

It's why we have tons of faith-based movies starring Dean Cain and Kevin Sorbo and why people will *still* argue that Tim Tebow could play quarterback in the NFL. If any of these men were nonpracticing, you would not remember their names; but because they profess Jesus, you most likely will continue hearing their names until the day you die.

All this to say, the incorporation of secular elements makes sense because their inclusion subconsciously projects credibility in a way that Christian culture doesn't superficially allow for and will not until there is a stylish Billy Graham sneaker corrolary to Yeezys or Jordans.

The modern evangelical church has a similar murky relationship with money. The prevailing sentiment is largely situationally based; in the hands of an unchurched individual, wealth is mostly mistrusted. But in the hands of a churched person or in a church fund for building expansions, suddenly money is welcomed.

This makes sense; historically, the church has had an almost habitual nebulousness when it comes to how money is spent. You can go back to the excesses of the Catholic church prior to the Protestant Reformation and see it today in the opulent and ostentatious megachurches dotting the landscape throughout the Bible Belt.

And that's to say nothing of lecherous televangelists operating with virtually no oversight or the philosophical scourge of the prosperity gospel, which seems to be less an ideology and more a predatory and exploitative scam aimed at the poor and undereducated.

My point: Isn't it ironic that the modern evangelical church is mostly agnostic when it comes to money?

That said, I do not mean to be willfully simplistic or to comprehensively villainize the historical and modern church as it relates to money. A large percentage of churches and organizations have done an incredible job with their tithes and offerings to ensure that they are responsible stewards with their money. Yet this dichotomy persists.

So what conclusion are we to arrive at given the established inconsistency of modern evangelical churches as it relates to money, materialism, and the low-key acceptance of secular culture? I don't know that there is a takeaway as much as we need to acknowledge that some things just are. For example, it's ideologically inconsistent for a pastor who claims to follow the lead of an impoverished Jewish refugee to then wear shoes that cost more than a thousand dollars. But it's also not fair to assume that this pastor isn't authentic or is somehow spiritually compromised because of his taste in fashion.

We can see a similar ideological inconsistency in the trend of "professional Christians" commoditizing their beliefs and acquiring followings and a certain status of celebrity based on their articulations of their faith. This commoditization has been slowly creeping into the platforms of prominent speakers, writers, and pastors who leverage the language of the Christian faith so comprehensively that the sacred vocabulary of the saints has been dangerously co-opted into empty platitudes that mostly function as a branding opportunity rather than as anything nearing a deeper understanding of God and belief. It seems inconsistent to professionalize an aspect of faith, but it happens, and it's almost impossible to objectively disentangle which occasions of this are good and which are bad.

On a micro level, I don't really care what pastors wear. I don't care what they spend their salaries on. It's their money and (hopefully) they earned it; if that means they spend a little more on something small or they want to spend money on incorporating various secular elements into their fashion, they should have the freedom to make that choice, understanding that they are also accountable for their choices to many more people than an average person is.

But on a macro level, I do very much care about the inconsistent and convenient application of when popular or secular culture is okay and when it is not, or when lavish wealth is determined to be keeping someone from a righteous lifestyle versus when it is romanced into being a key foundational element in the megachurch campus building campaign.

I'll confess that I find the PreachersNSneakers Instagram account to be much more necessary than most people would allow. For one, I find the ostentatious visual of pastors thirstily trying to court cultural relevancy to be eye-opening. For two, it's a reminder that while the issue of pastors in expensive shoes is a problem, the more urgent existential problem is about the institutional inconsistency in the modern evangelical church. And while those issues aren't as eye-catching as a professional Christian in some heated-up sneakers, they are begging Christians to do something about them.

TWENTY-EIGHT

THE MOURNFUL DETECTIVE

When Ashley and I found out she was pregnant with our third child, we decided to go the route of not knowing our baby's gender until it was born. This seemed like incredible fun and the logical thing for us to do given that our oldest child was a boy and our second child was a girl. Since we had our piece of the gender-ratio dream, why not just let the process surprise us and create a memorable experience?

In theory, this was good and rational and a great idea. But in reality, it was the absolute worst. Because even though you stipulate to yourself that you don't want to know the gender, you forget that you contain multitudes, and therefore the dormant detective buried deep within your psyche emerges intent on solving this self-imposed mystery. And the Sherlocknox Holmes that emerged was less a prodigy and more someone who just over-emphasized weird circumstantial evidence.

"I've noticed you're eating more Chick-fil-A this time around than you did with the last pregnancy, so I bet it's a boy."

"You were petting a boy dog at the park, and it sniffed you

intensely and tilted its head in the direction of your stomach, so it's totally a girl."

Also, this decision is the worst because you end up explaining to literally everyone you meet that you aren't finding out the gender, which is just the most painstakingly repetitive and horrific nightmare I could conjure up for myself. Welcome to small-talk and anecdotal hell.

Add to the worstness the reality that if the gender gets spoiled at any point in the pregnancy, it's a pretty huge mega-downer, and I can say that because I know from experience. This happened to us the day before Ashley was to be induced. *The day before.* Nine months of planning and . . . insert sad trombone noise here. I told myself that maybe we hadn't been spoiled, and it was just a mistake, and all our work the entire pregnancy wasn't completely down the drain, but we definitely had, and it definitely was.

The last reason contributing to the worstness, and to me the most important one, is the split reality you create for yourself.

Like I said earlier, even though I outwardly declared I wasn't going to find out, our minds don't obey whims like that, which is why Sherlocknox Holmes emerged. But I also began to mentally prepare for this child, whichever gender it emerged with. Part of that was just pragmatic; we needed two names at the ready. But also, there was no way I wasn't going to emotionally anticipate what each child's life would be like. Detailed futures and expectations were constructed, and there was not a single thought expended on what was going to happen to whichever future turned out to be the unreal one.

I could have never anticipated just how sad it was going to be to say goodbye to the idea of the child who would never come to fruition.

Our daughter Marlowe was born on April 16, 2014, and it was such a happy moment because she was just what our family needed—and she still is. It was a pretty seamless delivery,[1] and Marlowe was a beautiful and sweetly joyful baby.

But in the moment of meeting her, the experience was complicated by this other ceremony of sadness in parting with who she wasn't. I was forced to say goodbye to the tentative identity we'd created for her in case she was a boy. And it wasn't that we wanted a boy over a girl. We wanted whatever this baby ended up being, but unbeknownst to us, that was always going to end with us mourning someone.

Pennington (Penn) Lawrence McCoy wasn't born on April 16. Instead he just kind of floated away into the outer reaches of our consciousness until we stopped thinking about him. All our plans and hopes for him were permanently put on hold, never to be picked back up, which was weird when we'd spent so many months actively thinking about him as this potential person tethered directly to this other potential person.

To say that we had to mourn him feels wrong and rude and inappropriate; after all, we had Marlowe and were so completely head over heels for her. But we were left in this weird purgatory of not knowing how to mourn the loss of something that we never completely had.

Growing up, I was never told to dislike LGBTQ people. To non-Christians, it may seem like we get the "Not Liking LGBTQ

---

1. Ashley's words, not mine. I've been taught not to remark about the degree of difficulty in pushing a human out of a vagina until I do it myself.

People Talk" right alongside the "Sex Talk," but in my experience, it wasn't that overt. Understanding sex was mysterious, but knowing how to feel about anyone who fell outside the prescribed sexual boundaries was pretty straightforward. And I'm not speaking just as a Southern Baptist. The church was woefully behind on a lot of things—and still is, even in this moment—but the broader cultural attitude toward the LGBTQ community in the 1990s was just as inhospitable, maybe even more so. Kids like me may not have been super smart, but we were savvy to how the wind was blowing.

When I was in kindergarten, my teacher asked my parents if I was gay, because in gym class, when I rested between dodgeball throws, I held my arm at a ninety-degree angle to my side, with my hand hanging loosely down. And she wasn't asking because she was curious. It was a poorly veiled insult in the same way that as a teenager (and beyond) I would volley responses like "That's so gay" at my friends when I wanted to ridicule what they were doing.

Disapproval of LGBTQ people was so embedded into the foundation of who I was, it didn't even dawn on me to interrogate this idea. It was just an involuntary absolutism, because if both the church and culture could agree to the marginalization, then that group was obviously worthy of social exclusion.

This held up for a while because I never interacted with an LGBTQ person on a real-life level, and in pop culture the only gay or trans people I saw were such exaggerated versions that they didn't seem like real people—more like characters that life was asking them to play, thereby stripping them of an accessible humanity.

But the older I got, the more I began to cross paths with

people who are not straight or cisgender. And weirdly, when you are confronted with someone's humanity, it forces you to put away generalizations of how they should be and reconcile with how they actually are. Nothing will make you reconsider yourself more quickly than being faced with the person or people you've theoretically disagreed with or disapproved of your whole life.

Once the notion of someone being LGBTQ was humanized, I realized that I'd never really familiarized myself with the Bible verses that originated their presumptive sinfulness. I was so unaware of the scriptural source of this belief that I had to google it. I knew it was probably Leviticus and some other place, because Leviticus was the book about rules and boringness and, consequently, this is why Leviticus was always where my ambitions to read the entire Bible in one year went belly-up. But after Leviticus, I had no idea where else to look.

This was troubling to me. How did I have no idea where in the Bible these prohibitions were discussed? I tried to reassure myself that my ignorance of the locations of these anti-gay sentiments was proof of the transcendence of that belief, the idea being that internalizing something so thoroughly that I never even had to read the literature wasn't a failure of mine as much as it was a triumph of a belief so apparent that it need not be intentionally researched. But even a cursory glance at that kind of justification revealed that it was just the empty ramblings of a hypocrite.

Though this belief was reinforced through the casual and formal attitudes of those in and around the church, I realized that there was never any singular moment where I had opted in to it. There was a moment where I'd decided to follow Jesus, and there was a moment when I was baptized, and there was a moment when I chose to rededicate my life, but I was at a loss when trying to recall the moment when I'd decided to villainize a portion of the population for their sexual orientation or gender identity.

And that's when it dawned on me that trying to inventory the person you are requires you to reconsider certain aspects of your ideology—not just to reverse engineer how they came to be associated with you but to decide how you are going to proceed going forward.

So I began to wrestle with this belief. And once I was unencumbered by dogma and could look at the issue objectively, I immediately ran into three major issues.

1. I can't understand how homosexuality, if it appears throughout nature, can be called a choice. I never chose to be heterosexual; I just am. So why is this different for someone who is gay?

2. It felt simplistic to equate homosexuality with just another cross to bear, similar to how mine could be pride, selfishness, or gluttony with popcorn. As much as these issues are real things for me to overcome, they also don't compromise the essence of who I am. My saying yes to a gluttonous bucket of popcorn isn't complicated by it also being the only way I can find and express love in a committed relationship. It's just popcorn. But if homosexuality is a sin, then someone who is gay and also believes in Jesus has to live in the tension of believing something that denies them the ability to find companionship, love, and commitment. This felt particularly difficult to square away. I don't understand why God would make people gay and then ask them to endure the loneliness and marginalization associated with that.

3. Evangelical Christianity's conflict with the LGBTQ community seems motivated by its longstanding preoccupation
with sexuality. For my generation, reconciling the idea of
sexuality with faith has been particularly complicated
given a range of factors:

- the popularity of the True Love Waits movement (and
  the rise of purity culture) throughout the 1990s
- subinfluences like Joshua Harris's book *I Kissed Dating
  Goodbye*
- the Bill Clinton / Monica Lewinsky scandal (which,
  given that it involved sex and a president largely
  villainized by most evangelical Christians, you cannot
  overestimate how singular this event was in the
  continued stigmatization of sex)

The unintended consequences of these influences is a vacuum in the understanding of sexuality and a compulsion to avoid
verbalizing that misunderstanding.

Throughout my high school years, my time in purity culture
emphasized and isolated virginity and avoiding premarital sex
as the most important things, and it accomplished this to the
detriment of every other nuance around sexuality, specifically
the physical, emotional, and spiritual purposes of sex within a
marriage. Somehow we were supposed to avoid sex at all costs,
but once we were married we were expected to be chastened
porn stars who were capable of satisfying and understanding
our partners completely. This head-in-the-sand approach to sexuality also extends to non-straight sexual orientations; it distills
them down to the "unnatural" component, to say nothing of

any other aspect of the love and commitment that exist within these relationships.

From these initial hesitations I tree-limbed onto the two broad but very necessary reconsiderations I had to attempt. First was about the general Christian stance toward our LGBTQ neighbors. This was fairly obvious, as any person who actively believes in Jesus cannot think that our treatment of LGBTQ people has been in any way compliant with the WWJD cliché. The hatred, rejection, vitriol, and judgment we reserve for them is in no way commensurate with the interpreted scriptural offense. We are flippant about divorce and infidelity, and pastors who admit sexual impropriety and abuse of power bear that shame for a microscopic amount of time, yet our endurance for demonizing people who are not straight or cis is incredible. This resilience in marginalizing a portion of the population is not without precedent for evangelicals. Though the evangelical movement is around only 150 years old, a development close to our origin story was rallying around segregation in the post–Civil War world. Not a great look to be sure, but one I would hope that we could learn from.

Luckily, I think many modern evangelicals *are* learning from this and are feeling the necessity of reconsidering our beliefs. But many others are feeling the pressure to double down on their positions and reline their already lined positions in the sand.

And I understand this! I think a failure of modern discourse is that when we evolve or change or reconsider, we expect everyone around us to immediately do the same. When they don't, we express frustration or, worse, use hyperbolic language to shame them for not being as "enlightened" or "woke" as we are. But we are all different people with different experiences moving through life at different speeds. While the hope is that we can all eventually arrive at an understanding of what the common good is, we are crazy if we don't realize that this happens at a different, unique speed for everyone, if it happens at all.

This relates directly to the second reconsideration: for something as important as sexual orientation and considering how tethered it is to identity, I don't think it's enough for Christians to generalize the entirety of their belief based off the six verses that address it. That in no way is meant to diminish those verses, but as with many parts of the Bible, we have to get beyond just hearing the words and move more into considering the spirit of those words, their contexts, the audiences they were spoken to, and their historical motives. I know how wishy-washy that directive can sound, but this topic deserves thoughtful, nuanced study, just like any other we'd consult the Bible on.

It's not easy to consider these issues. I'll be transparent and say that I wrestled with writing about this topic. My trepidation is not because it feels like I might be unraveling my faith but because within certain Christian circles, questioning traditional thinking comes with a stigma attached. You're forced to whisper the words in conversation, and even then, you can only bring it up in front of people you trust. Not because the topic is controversial but because we've been conditioned to see the topic as controversial—so much so that we're willing to villainize and diminish fellow Christians who think differently.[2]

This is wild because, as you can probably tell, there are a handful of ways I think differently than many other Christians. That doesn't mean that I hold them in less regard or villainize

---

2. *cough* Jen Hatmaker *cough*

them (and I expect that they extend me the same courtesy); on the contrary, I think we are all the product of different experiences that shape our worldviews and our connections to God. If we were honest with ourselves, I think we'd agree that we're all passengers on an ever-changing journey of understanding this life, ourselves, and how we interpret God, and we have to get out of the mind-set that to recognize this is wrong or disobedient. It isn't.

It would be completely disingenuous for me to write this chapter and not at least mildly delineate where I've landed. After all, if the entire purpose of this book is to show you how the belief sausage[3] is made within my own head, why pull up on this particular issue, one that it appears, at least anecdotally, a generation of Christians are already either organically reconsidering or feeling the impetus to do so?

After reading and researching and listening to biblical scholars much, much more intelligent than myself, I've come to believe that homosexuality isn't a sin. We don't blanket-identify heterosexuality as a sin; I think we can't do that with homosexuality either. Heterosexuality has iterations that are good (a committed, loving relationship) and iterations that are bad (prostitution, infidelity, abuse). We would never diminish all of heterosexuality because of these bad iterations, and to do this to homosexuality feels incorrect.

The tension of this chapter for me is wanting to tell you exactly what I think and what I've learned about every verse I've studied and why I believe what I believe while also recognizing that I'm in the bottom 10 percent of people academically and spiritually trained to do that. That said, I'm including my reading list in a

---

3. I thought I would regret typing "belief sausage," but I'm actually feeling great about it.

footnote[4] so you can see some of the literature I accessed while reconsidering this issue.

Broadly though, I'll say that my (and others') interpretation of the Old Testament verses is that the concept of homosexuality as reflected in the Bible is much different from what it means today. For example, I interpret the verses about homosexuality in Leviticus to be less about all humanity and more focused on priestly purification for the Levites and the Israelites at large, as they were intended to be intermediaries between God and the world after their exodus from Egypt. Regarding Sodom and Gomorrah, I believe the often-shared interpretation of the cities' destruction as punishment for homosexual activity is an over-simplification caught up in the modern association of sodomy with homosexuality, which doesn't have anything to do with God's actual motivation for the destruction.

I believe the New Testament verses concerning homosexuality are complicated by the translation choices modern scholars have made and that the societal scourge of pederasty[5] at the time these verses were written informed the inclusion of the language that we would later understand to refer to homosexuality.

We can dive much deeper into these verses, but at the risk of taking on a linguistic and interpretative journey I'm not qualified to take, I'll leave it there with the understanding that this is less a delineation of beliefs and more a thumbnail sketch of where my reconsideration took me.

I know the above is simultaneously a lot and not enough as

---

4. *Messy Grace* by Caleb Kaltenbach, *UnClobber* by Colby Martin, *Changing Our Mind* by David Gushee, *Gay Girl, Good God* by Jackie Hill Perry.
5. A socially acknowledged romantic relationship between an adult male and a younger male, usually in his teens.

it pertains to this topic, but I hope this somewhat ratifies my reconsideration as something done less out of feelings and cultural influence and more as the product of intellectual analysis. But even more, my intention is that it spurs you to do your own reconsideration. Again, let me repeat the mantra of this book: my wish and purpose isn't to tell you exactly what to think but rather to show you my process in hopes that it will inform your own. Where you land in those reconsiderations is for you to decide.

To that point, I'll leave you with this encouragement. Historically there is an intellectual diversity in Christian belief, but the modern contrast to that is how Christianity has gotten more polarized. The net effect is that anything that challenges the insular bubble of accepted mainstream Christianity isn't just wrong, it's also an enemy of the faith. An enemy of God, even. But the Bible and our beliefs about what it teaches have to be more than just a rhetorical argument point. They have to be something we understand—not only their essence and their connection to God but the context of their origin and how that affects how we put those beliefs into tangible practice.

Faithfulness requires criticism and consideration and doubt; otherwise how can you be sure that your belief is valid?

In other words, you may read these words and disagree with me and assume that I'm a godless heretic dedicated to subverting God or attacking a specific aspect of your faith. But, truly, I'm honoring my faith and attempting to deconstruct it to the point that I can understand it and abide in it, not out of *thoughtlessness* but out of *thoughtfulness*.

To me, faith demands the reconsiderations of doubt. It is our obligation to not be so lazy in our faith that we forget to doubt but also to not be so lazy in our doubt that we forget to build an actual and realized faith.

Just as Ashley and I departed with the idea of a son we were never meant to have, sometimes as believers we have to depart with the beliefs and ideas we absorb without choice.

It can be a difficult mourning process, to depart with such beliefs, but it is one made easier with the knowledge that we never really had them in the first place. Why lament something that never was when you can truly celebrate what actually is?

TWENTY-NINE

PRAYER

Of all the things entangled with what I believe, the one that has vexed me the most is prayer.

As a child, praying was easy. I'm convinced that prayer is at its most understandable when you are young because you're already used to appealing to a higher power for everything you want or need. It's just part of the deal.

You want to mix your own chocolate milk? Parents need to green-light that.

You want to bring in your pet rock for show-and-tell? The teacher needs to approve that.

You want to skip a varsity baseball game to go to prom with your girlfriend from a different high school? Coach needs to sign off first.

But the older you get, the more agency you have, and you lose the rhythm of asking. See, even that feels like a primitive understanding of prayer, because I'm just talking about it in terms of what we ask of God. That's the whole problem I run into: I have no idea how prayer works or if I'm doing it right.

In this moment, my impulse is to deflect and assume a defensive posture about how this is my fault and I'm the problem. And it's not that I don't think that; I pretty much do. But it feels deceptive to talk in these self-critical terms, because my misunderstanding of prayer isn't for a lack of trying.

I've prayed fervently and diligently, and the concept of prayer has long been embedded deep within the bedrock of what I believe to be true about my faith. But sometimes, when those things are so deeply embedded, you forget what they mean, if you ever even knew in the first place.

My initial experience with prayer is that it was a hotline to God. You need something, kick it up to God. If he can do it, he'll do it. If he doesn't, then it wasn't that he couldn't; it was just some other priority probably preempting the request.

Which right there is a problem for someone like me. I need to understand the why, good or bad, and the idea that a prayer request hadn't received a binary yes or no was tough for me to grasp—and it still is. There seemed to be so many intangible complications that threatened to undo the entire structure:

What if I didn't model my prayer after the Lord's Prayer? Does that mean it never floated beyond my roof?

What if the answer wasn't a yes or a no, but a "not right now"?

What if there was an answer, but I just couldn't see it then—or ever?

As a kid, the idea of the prayer matrix God was having to sift through was immensely overwhelming, which was in such contrast to the simplicity of the mechanism. Prayer was just so simple and easy, and I loved this aspect as a kid because it was one of the few things about my faith that I felt confident I wasn't screwing up. But once my prayers entered into the cosmic chain of command, then what happened?

How a prayer has to be funneled, considered, processed, and resolved was incredibly unclear to me then, and that hasn't changed now. It's the problem with worshiping a supernatural God but attempting to understand him in a human construct. Our projection of how it all works is never going to be accurate, and that's making the wild assumption that it's even within our capacity to intellectually quantify any part of the process. But then again, that's all we have, and so we keep at it.

In this sense, it's like me at a dance during a fast song. I can only do the robot.[1] When you can only do the robot, you just robot and hope that it can approximate the effect you are wanting for the duration of the song. And once I tried to understand prayer on an intellectual level, that's what it felt like—me just horrifically doing the spiritual robot and hoping it was close enough to the real thing.

As I tried to better wrap my head around prayer, I built intellectual scaffolding around platitudes about prayer that I routinely ran across at church. None of these solved the problem, but they help me approximate the idea a bit more.

Platitude 1: Ask and Ye Shall Receive

I loved this one because it streamlined the whole process. You basically just had to fill out the proper spiritual paperwork. Very

---

1. I can't do the robot. I don't know why I'm claiming I can. I'm trying to make a larger point, but this is a brazen lie—do not believe me.

quickly though, I put it together that this idea either wasn't true or was wildly oversimplified. Because if it were true that you received what you asked for, what was to differentiate God from the genie in *Aladdin*?

"Ask and ye shall receive" seemed to push this idea that God was some kind of divine being more devoted to playing fetch with us, in the form of requests and hopes, than he was to governing the cosmos. I may not have known much as a young Christian, but I knew enough to surmise that there was more to prayer than transactions. After all, God was, you know, God. Not a Jimmy John's employee.

Platitude 2: It's All Part of God's Plan

We've all heard the cliché trotted out about how "God has a plan" or "It's all part of the plan." This idea suggests a divine blueprint as the behavioral foundation behind what we are doing in this life. Even if it wasn't explicitly stated to us in a cliché like this, we intuitively buy into this idea given what we read in the Bible. Creation occurred, but then sin happened. This led to separation from God, which eventually led to Jesus. I know I just yadda-yadda-ed the entire Bible, but it's in service to a bigger point: If we accept this Big Plan idea, how do our moment-to-moment prayers intersect with it?

Is the Big Plan contingent on our prayers happening to spur it forward, or does it exist above and beyond our prayers? *Or* does it exist in concert with our prayers, having already incorporated them because God foreknew[2] that they were going to be prayed prior to us even being alive?

---

2. Is *foreknew* even a word? I really hope so because after typing it, I pretty much fell in love with it.

Can you see how quickly this scrambled my brain? Even now I'm conflicted about whether to delete the entire previous paragraph in an effort to try to explain my thinking more succinctly, but that line of thinking truly does illustrate my confusion.

And like anyone else, when I'm confused my tendency is to become evasive. This is especially true in the pages of a book where I'm supposed to be the self-assured author charioting you to revelations like how you should wash your face more and apologize less.

I'll be honest with you: I'm feeling a lot of shame in this chapter. I'm pretty self-conscious and insecure about essentially being like, "How do I do a pray?" But these questions are my questions, and while their presence isn't proof of a flaw, it is proof of a deeper disturbance within my understanding that is begging to be excavated.

Platitude 3: I Just Want God's Will for My Life

I've prayed this so many times, but every time I said it, the words were more out of rehearsed rhetoric and less out of thinking it through. And no shade to you if you say this, because it might be an Ebenezer[3] for you or emblematic of some larger and deeper connective tissue to your faith. But for me it's devoid of meaning, because all I can think about is God hearing my prayer and then turning to a control room like NASA: HEAVEN and being like, "You guys, he's given us the green light!" And then sixty white

---

3. Not like an Ebenezer Scrooge but rather something symbolic to us or reminding of God's presence in our lives. Though theoretically, Ebenezer Scrooge could accommodate this Ebenezer duality in the right conditions.

men celebrate wildly because evidently those are the only people who work at NASA, if we are to believe movies about space.

Obviously, my conflict with this statement is that God's will for my life seems to be coming whether I want it or not, but using this as a qualifier after I've made a request of God always feels like a move meant to manipulate him more than honor him.

INT. HEAVEN BOARDROOM

God and Underling are going through the business of the day in a very stylish boardroom featuring glass walls and a long meeting table with delicious pastries on it. Underling presents God with the necessary paperwork to execute the necessities of life on earth.

GOD

All right, next request. *(scans the paperwork briefly)* So this one wants his dad to not have cancer. Which is great. Very good use of a prayer request, not going to lie.

HEAVEN UNDERLING

I agree. The only problem is that your will for his life was for him to lose his dad to cancer.

GOD

(sighs heavily) Wow, really? That was my will?

HEAVEN UNDERLING

Your initials are right here.

(God looks. We see "YHWH" on the paperwork.)

GOD

Uggggggggggh. Could we push it back? Like maybe a couple of years?

HEAVEN UNDERLING

Unfortunately, it says that you wanted it here for "the good of those who love the Lord's purposes."

GOD

Remind me what that meant in this circumstance?

HEAVEN UNDERLING

Hmm, let me check the notes. It says you wanted it here so that it would emotionally shape him for future purposes. He's particularly spiritually tender now, so it really has to happen on schedule.

GOD

Wait. Hold your horses and the phone and all the other things that require holding.

HEAVEN UNDERLING

What, what is it? Are they rebooting *90210* again? It doesn't even make sense without Luke Perry (RIP).

GOD

No, I forgot to keep reading the prayer request. At the end of his request, he clarified that he really does just want my will to be done.

(God holds up the paperwork and reveals a folded-under portion that they both missed.)

HEAVEN UNDERLING

Say no more, fam. I didn't know we had a God's-will enthusiast on our hands.

(Reggae horns play on the speakers and confetti explodes. Underling crumples up Dad's cancer death certificate.)

Kobe![4] *(tosses it into a nearby trash can)*

---

4. RIP, Mamba. Gone too soon.

```
I'm rescheduling that cancer death
for three years from now.

                GOD

You know what? Make it five. No! Make
it freaking never.

          HEAVEN UNDERLING

Freaking never it is!

(They freeze-frame high-five.)
```

Obviously, this isn't how things go down in heaven, for a lot of reasons. For example, they definitely are a paperless society.

But even more apparent to me was that despite being armed with clichés, I was still not getting any closer to understanding prayer. So I just kind of stopped.

If I didn't know the point, then what sense did it make to arbitrarily and emptily recite words? I certainly interacted with the ritual of prayer in the context of church, and my evangelical guilt compelled me to routinely sprinkle some generic prayers out there. But every time I tried something authentic and genuine, I felt like the person in a conversation who can't hear too well but tries to lip-read what the other person is saying, which always leads to a missed joke, or worse, an emphatic LOL after a tragic revelation.[5]

As a parent I would pray with my kids, but even here I felt a smidge guilty. Why was I pushing them into this behavior if I myself didn't know what to make of it? Isn't parenting about

---

5. Ashley is one of these people. She has the hearing of a 340-year-old person. If you ever talk to her, 60 percent of the time she's trying to read your lips.

shepherding your kids into behaviors and habits that you yourself have appropriately grasped first?

And isn't that a commentary in and of itself? The continued and prolonged doing of something, even if its effects are negligible, is so much more palatable than just not doing it.

My stopping prayer wasn't an act of rebellion or symptomatic of a larger dissatisfaction with God. I just didn't know how to do it because I didn't know what it meant.

Contributing to this conflict was the later realization that I had a poor foundational understanding of who God was—so how was I also supposed to intimately communicate with him? Added to that, I'm not really what you would call a talker, and I'm wired to feel shameful about asking for help. In a lot of ways, me praying was like trying to catch a marble with a Hula-Hoop: just a star-crossed pursuit destined for failure, which foreshadowed my time away from prayer as less a reaction and more an eventuality.

Sometimes you have to remove something to allow yourself to understand the deeper meaning beyond the familiarity and clichés that surround it. Once I removed prayer as a box to check, I began to experience connection with God in a variety of ways that were decidedly unprayerful.

I found this connection in works of art. Stories, songs, pictures and the like, none explicitly addressing the concept of God, yet all of them evoking something that pushed me into contemplation of him.

I found this in exercise. There was something meditative about the repetitive motion of movement that freed my mind up to wander and wonder.

I found this in my work. In 2017, we launched a second podcast called *The Bible Binge*, where we aimed to recap the Bible as if it were a book, movie, or TV show. We never intended for it to be a supplement to my or other people's spiritual development, but this nontheologian, everyman/everywoman approach to the Bible ended up being deeply affecting for me as a sort of public auditing of what I believed, what I didn't believe, and what I wasn't sure of.

It seemed prayer had been a barrier for me all along, because I misunderstood the entire point from the very beginning. It wasn't a daily list of requisitions or a mandated rundown of my day. It wasn't something I was required to do before meals and bedtime and after devotions. It was a ritual aimed not at contouring things as I wanted them to be but at my heart and how it needed to be for my actions to reflect my principles.

I don't think prayer is about requests. I don't think it's about changing the heart of God. I think prayer is about changing my own heart and using the occasion and ceremony of the moment to just listen. To God. To myself. To each other. To the bigger picture going on around us. And whether that picture is part of the plan or God's will for my life or neither, I honestly have no idea. But what I do know is that it finally feels like I have another move to do besides the spiritual robot.

THIRTY

WHAT KEEPS YOU?

Recently, I reread the story of the exodus, which, outside of the resurrection, is probably the most incredibly wild story in the Bible. It's simultaneously an origin story and a revenge story, populated by supernatural elements.

Naturally, when I read Exodus, I always think of the end of *The Godfather*:

- Both creatively and unexpectedly elevate an untraditional central character: Moses / Michael Corleone.
- The climactic sequences of both stories work to definitively settle all outstanding feuds or debts: with Pharaoh and the Egyptians / with Barzini, Tattaglia, Cuneo, Stracci, Moe Greene, and Tessio.
- Each one lays a strong enough foundation[1] to support the stories built out from it: the rest of the Bible / *The Godfather: Parts II and III.*

---

1. *Hamilton* reference.

And lastly, these stories are related by how they use elements of fiction and nonfiction. Hear me out.

———

When you want to figure out what you think about something, sometimes it's important to make yourself aware of all the different ways you can think about it.

For example, some modern scholars view Exodus as an origin story fashioned together more to provide an ideology and cultural identity than to recount a literal history. This is because, in a world where Israel has been destabilized, a historical identity is existentially urgent.

Other scholars argue that the story as it appears in the Bible is literal fact.

And yet other groups of scholars think it's a combination of the two.

I should say that I've never been confused for a scholar. If you've made it to this point in the book, you know that. I won't pretend to be one now, but when it comes to squaring this story with what I think, what I believe, and what I defer to scientifically and archaeologically, I think I land somewhere in the middle.

Is it weird that the elements that give me the most intellectual hesitance are exactly zero of the supernatural aspects?

God afflicting Egypt with the plagues or appearing to Moses as a burning bush? All in. God's physical manifestation existing as a pillar of cloud in the day and a pillar of fire at night with which to guide the Israelites across the desert? Sign me up. These things give me no pause because my particular belief about God is that the more you think you can quantify his behavior and activity within human logic and reason, the less you have an actual supernatural deity and the more you have some malleable concept of what God should or should not do.

No, my hesitation was always in how there is no archeological evidence of the Israelites living in Egypt during this time. Also, the numbers of the Israelites in Egypt rely on some creative bookkeeping. (For example, Rashi's commentary on the Torah interprets claims that all the Israelite women in Egypt were giving birth to only sextuplets.)

Even then, mathematically, the 2.5 million Israelites said to have existed, plus their livestock, would have taken much more than one night to cross the Red Sea.

I'm going to stop here because you get the point: there are aspects of the exodus story that may not be exactly, literally true. But I'm also stopping because the guilt is encroaching on my words, as though they are a sacrilege trying to hatchet away this belief system to which I willingly ascribe. If I start pulling on some threads of doubt, where does it go? And will the whole thing come undone?

That's a huge, complicated question, and by no means should we simplify it or diminish it. Doubts and questions require this duality of balance: they are to be encouraged but also interrogated, and if you skew too far in either direction, you can quickly lose the handle on what you are trying to accomplish.

The balance of belief and doubt is too complicated to generalize, so I won't. But I can speak to the specific balancing act I'm attempting.

If God appeared to me tomorrow and confirmed every sentence of Exodus as literal fact, nothing in my belief would fundamentally change. (Except, you know, God literally appearing to me would be pretty bonkers.)

Conversely, if God appeared and wrote off the entire exodus story as the founding myths of a national identity, that wouldn't really change anything for me either.

Neither of these options would destabilize my faith. Not because I'm Kirk Cameron or some kind of religious wunderkind; it's more because the specific details and contours of Bible stories are not what keep me. Again, I want to reiterate that this isn't what I think should be true for you as much as it is my accounting for what keeps me believing what I believe. Because God knows how much I've wrestled with all this.

I often contend with standing on the border between belief and nihilism. I'm just prone to it. Some people are born being able to roll their tongues like Cardi B.[2] Others are given tendencies toward generosity of spirit. Unfortunately, I was bequeathed with the talent for feeling drawn toward the abyss of "nothing matters and nothing is true." Aren't you jealous? This is where you should be very jealous of me.

When I am in this mind-set, I can talk myself out of everything. I can find piercing doubt at every turn, and I can see my faith as a thin and paltry layer of protection against the dread.

In these moments I think of the chorus from Derek Webb's song "Wedding Dress" wherein he calls himself a whore and likens faith and belief to the act of putting on a wedding dress despite not being pure or faithful.

I think of this song because in these moments, I'm convinced

---

2. My kids and I all can, but not Ashley. However, we gracefully accept her flaw in this regard and never taunt her about it (not!).

that I have faith only in the ornamental sense. That I trot it out only when I need to showcase it to myself or others or both, but ultimately, most truly and essentially, I'm just prostituting the belief of something bigger into a kind of comfort for myself that can't really exist as I believe it to.

I don't know why I have the tendency to do this. Is it because I value knowledge and understanding, but when you collide this impulse with something inherently un-understandable (God), the trickle-down effect is an unreconcilable tension?

Is it because I've correctly but tragically realized that life is pointless?

Or maybe it's that this tendency toward dread is my affliction because only the effort of trying to defeat it can eventually bring me to a more transcendent understanding of what God is, who God is, and what my purpose in connection to God is?

Truly and deeply, when I am living in harmony with both my head and heart, I don't believe that everything is nothing, so I have to tether myself to what I believe to be true about my faith— the things that supplement this certainty when I am thinking most clearly.

These elements and beliefs are the tent poles holding up the canvas of my faith. They are the incontrovertible things that I can't outthink or out-rationalize even at my most nihilistic and cynical.

For example, maybe the Red Sea was literally parted, or maybe not. Maybe there were literally 2.5 million Israelites who crossed it, or maybe there weren't. The degree to which these stories contain embellishments or are bedrocks of history makes utterly no difference to me.

But what *does* make a difference is that something like

Exodus was written centuries before the birth of Jesus, and yet it so heavily foreshadows and sets up the redemption narrative arc that is threaded throughout the Bible and ultimately satisfied by Jesus. It may sound silly, but that narrative harmony is one of the things that keeps me from floating toward the abyss.

Maybe you don't struggle with abyss-adjacent thoughts, or maybe it's never dawned on you to think about what keeps you believing what you believe.

Or maybe, like me, you struggle every day, and there is a tiny little piece of you too afraid to pull at the patchwork of what you believe for fear of the mess you might make.

Wherever you land, I can speak from experience that, as complicated as it might seem, it's worth reconsidering your belief. That reconsideration is the difference between a faith that is for display purposes only and one that can lead you out of captivity.

CONCLUSION

So we've reached the end of our journey of reconsideration. This is where you watch your step, gather all your belongings, and disembark from the book because we've appropriately celebrated reconsideration to the point where you probably never ever want to hear that word again. And listen, I get it. I do. For me, *reconsider* has become one of those words that, if you say it enough, becomes a blob of meaningless sounds, like *fahrvergnügen* or Jeremy Renner's newest musical album.

So I appreciate your allowing me to inundate your consciousness with a word that inherently feels like more trouble than you need.

I hope your takeaway is not feeling overwhelmed by constantly having to reconsider everything, always, no matter how simple, but rather feeling the freedom, agency, and initiative to figure out why you believe what you believe. Remember, the point of reconsideration isn't to complicate or confuse; it's to clarify.

I'm so passionate about this point that if I had a gong or a reggae horn, I would play it here. As a matter of fact, that's definitely happening in the audio version of this book, so just know that the previous sentence resonated for audiobook listeners in a big way.

I began this book talking about a dog with a crossbow, and

we will end it talking about an elephant with a laser-beam cannon. I'm kidding. I don't even know if a laser-beam cannon is a weaponizable thing, and elephants are notoriously passive when it comes to extraskeletal weaponry. Just look at Babar.[1]

We will end this book talking about *Hamilton*, the smash-hit musical from the incomparable Lin-Manuel Miranda. He is so dedicated to goodness and the general emotional enrichment of our culture that I would consider cutting off one of my pinky fingers if it meant adding one year to his life.

As you no doubt have noticed, I've been almost obnoxious in my shoehorning of *Hamilton* lyrics into this book. I would apologize, but I have no real regret about it. In writing, you will invariably have darlings. You will be forced to kill some of them and maim others, but—if you are truly lucky—some of your literary darlings will reach full maturity. *Hamilton* references were the self-indulgent darlings of this book, and I do appreciate your toleration, especially if you haven't seen *Hamilton*.

But now that the book is behind us, I want to explain all the references and why they were so important to me. For starters, the character of Alexander Hamilton and the soundtrack of the musical dedicated to his life were a constant-yet-distant companion to me in the process of writing. I tried to include a chapter specifically about Hamilton in forty-eight different ways, but it just never made sense within the bigger theme of the book. This was particularly frustrating for me because, as I was writing this book, *Hamilton* was the artistic influence of record. To not be able to corral that influence into content felt like a failure.

---

1. The word *notorious* is doing a lot of work here, as there is no scientific evidence to corroborate this beyond the "it feels right" sensibility that motivated the original intent.

Seeing this book on the other side,[2] I realize why it never worked.

The bigger and more appropriate application of *Hamilton* was meant to exist here in the conclusion. So if you'll indulge me one last time,[3] I'll thread this idea together.

From the beginning of the musical, a contentious dynamic is set up between Alexander Hamilton and Aaron Burr (spoiler alert: he eventually murders Hamilton) both because of the eventual crescendo of their conflict and because, fundamentally, they see the world in different ways.

Both are orphaned, but Burr's orphaning comes with a lonely privilege and overwhelming sense of having to live up to a legacy he is detached from. The idea of reconsideration is strong within Burr because he's constantly having to hold the legacy of his family up against who he is and who he wants to be.

Conversely, there is an absence of legacy surrounding Hamilton and almost no expectation for his future accomplishments. Accordingly, Hamilton doesn't waste effort on reconsideration, because he is nothing and he has nothing.

These framings tell us everything we need to know about each character. Because of these influences and origins, Hamilton is precocious, gritty, and ambitious whereas Burr is equivocating and overly patient to the point of timidity.

As the musical progresses, the two characters do intellectual and political battle with increasing frequency. Their conflicting ideologies culminate in the fateful duel that eventually claims Hamilton's life and dooms Burr to a historical legacy as the butt-head who shot perhaps the most brilliant American financial

---

2. *Hamilton* reference.
3. *Hamilton* reference.

mind to ever live—an unsatisfactory conclusion for both the real men and the characters within the musical.

Conclusions aside, the intermingling of these characters and their motivations was always at the heart of my vision for this book. (When it was just one set of footprints in the sand, it was Lin-Manuel Miranda carrying me, etc.)

Burr exists as a metaphor for the stability of conventional wisdom, tradition, and status quo. Hamilton is a metaphor for the positive upheaval and chaos that revolution can bring. Neither of these are inherently bad, but as we see in the development of both characters, they both become corrosive when they exist without balancing each other. Balance was always the hope and heart of this book.

As kids we're conditioned to accept what is presented to us, but as adults it's less clear how to proceed. Is it wrong to reconsider? Are verification and scrutinization indicative of something negative or just the due diligence of a better understanding?

When we're faced with divergent paths, our compulsion can be to stop and hold steady, like an Aaron Burr figure, waiting for a definitive and safer clarity to be delineated for us. The flip side is to reject everything. Be outraged by all the things, lament all the traditions, and assume that our only hope is in rejecting the foundation of everything that came before. I don't know about you, but both options sound exhausting.

At the end of the song in which Burr recounts killing Hamilton, he laments that he should've known that the world was wide enough for both Hamilton and himself, and I find that to be a fitting note to end this book on.

The world is wide enough for us to not always know exactly what we think.

The world is wide enough for us to disagree with each other without resorting to petty dismissiveness.

And the world within ourselves—our minds, hearts, and beliefs—is wide enough to accommodate both hanging back to thoughtfully preserve our traditions and experiences and charging forward with the boldness of reconsideration in the pursuit of better understanding.

ACKNOWLEDGMENTS

While I concede that mostly no one cares how the book-writing sausage gets made, I'm still going to comment upon it regardless, because this is my book, and I'm feeling particularly megalomaniacal in this moment.

I'll be straight with you: writing this book was a very lonely process. It was imposed upon me when I wasn't ready to write it, by people I didn't really work much with, and at a time where I was going through a lot of personal tumult. But when there was only one set of footprints in the sand, I realize now that this book was what was carrying me.

Just kidding. That was a joke just now.

But in all seriousness, the urgency of writing this book and the loneliness connected to it is something that will always be weirdly special to me. I don't know how else to write that without it sounding melodramatic, but it's true, so whatever. Don't be weird.

Very specific and special thanks to:

- Amtrak. I wrote most of this book riding a train back and forth from Birmingham to New Orleans. Along with gaining the original draft of this book, I gained a newfound appreciation for train rides because they are dope, and

I highly recommend taking one, especially if you have a deadline.

- New Orleans. You are loud, dirty, mysterious, and the perfect setting for frenetic writing. For this, you will always be a special place to me in a way that most people cannot understand.
- Suzanne Stabile. Your work helped me in specific chapters of this book, but even more, in life.
- Lin-Manuel Miranda, for aforementioned, obvious, and Hamiltonian reasons.
- The unaware members of the soundtrack behind the writing of this book: Andrew Bird, Nicholas Britell, Jonny Greenwood, Nick Cave and Warren Ellis, Johnnyswim, and Explosions in the Sky.
- Shia LaBeouf. In many ways, your ethos is my muse.
- Meaghan Porter, for taking my words and making them better.
- Jamie Golden, Erin Moon, Jason Waterfalls, Christiana Hill, Jordan Gordon-Levitt, Vance Maldonaldo, and everyone else associated with The Popcast Media Group. As a kid, I didn't know what podcasting was, but if I had, TPMG would have been my dream job, both for the work we get to do and for the kind of people I get to do that work with. Y'all the real MVPs.
- Mom, Dad, and Laura, for knowing me like you know me and still associating with me.
- Rowe, Sidda Gray, and Marlowe. This book will all make more sense when you are older. I hope.
- Ashley. I'll never forget those nights by the pool when we would talk about some of the difficult and more

complicated stuff in this book. I can still see you now, sitting in that patio chair, asking me hard questions with your head in your hands while I floated in the water, sometimes disappearing below the surface, because I didn't always know what to say.

Thank you for your grace in giving me space to write, your partnership in helping me think through what to write, and your love for always being exactly what I needed. Even when I disappear below the surface for a bit.

ABOUT THE AUTHOR

KNOX MCCOY loves laughing and making people laugh. Really, anything that's laughter-adjacent, he's into. He's also super into the word *swashbuckling*, and his dream is to one day use it in a bio.

Knox began podcasting in 2011 as a way to talk more about popular culture, and to his extreme surprise, he's still doing that via *The Popcast with Knox and Jamie* and *The Bible Binge*.

As a resident of the South, Knox's heritage is to enjoy football and barbecue, and he does so with great passion. He also enjoys zombie movies, police procedurals, and a good Netflix binge.

Knox lives in Birmingham, Alabama, with his wife, three kids, and basset hound, Luna Lovegood. There, he works as the swashbuckling cofounder of The Popcast Media Group.

What do you get when you mix pop culture, faith, and a hint of nostalgia?

In his first book, *The Wondering Years*, podcaster Knox McCoy tells hilarious stories about how pop culture helped him answer life's biggest questions. Dive into a witty and winsome exploration of the ways our favorite stories, characters, and conflicts continue to influence our lives.

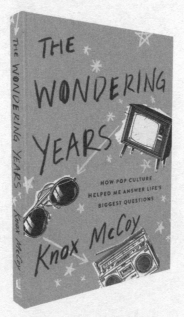

Available wherever books and ebooks are sold

For more information, visit
KnoxMcCoy.com

THE WONDERING YEARS

Introduction

On Introductions

I gotta say, as a society we have really lost our way when it comes to introductions. It's all lede-burying and the transfer of non-essential information.

A typical introduction goes something like, "Hello, I'm Duane. I work in IT." Think about that. What do we know about Duane now? Basically his name and his job, two things that 92 percent of Americans report being dissatisfied with.[1]

And I'm going to admit to you that I have no idea what IT even means. Something about technology or computers, probably. Intrepid Technologer? Illuminati Taskforce? I dunno. Sure, I could google it and find out, but that would take effort and I just don't care that much. Which is the essence of modern-day introductions: no one cares that much.

You know who does introductions right? People on *Game of Thrones*. Specifically the show's central figure, Daenerys Targaryen. Listen to the impression she makes with her title: *Daenerys Stormborn of the House Targaryen, First of Her Name,*

---

1. Not a real stat. But it *feels* like a real stat, no?

the Unburnt, Queen of the Andals and the First Men, Khaleesi of the Great Grass Sea, Breaker of Chains, and Mother of Dragons.

That is such a satisfying introduction it should probably come with a cigarette. We get a lot of stuff we can figure out (example: she probably can't be burnt, I'm assuming?) as well as some stuff we need more info on ("So, Daenerys, tell me more about these dragons you mother. What's their thing? What are they about?")

Bottom line: It's a great introduction because it entertains, informs, and gives tons of material regarding who she is and what she's about. Quite a bit better than "Duane from IT," right?

Let's look at another great introduction: the theme song of *The Fresh Prince of Bel-Air.* It is sonically pleasing *and* it provides the foundational context of the show. In the span of a couple of minutes, we get the following info:

- Will grew up and came to physical maturity in West Philadelphia.
- There, he was often found spending his days on the playground.
- This was the setting for one skirmish with such ominous forebodings that his mother feared for Will's safety.
- Therefore, she put him in a taxicab and sent him from Philadelphia to Bel-Air.[2]

That's an entire origin story delivered concisely, delightfully, and expertly by the lead character. It only makes sense that you'd want to watch the episode to follow.

---

2. Does it matter that the cab ride would have meant Will rode approximately 2,750 miles? It's called suspension of disbelief, you guys.

One last example of introductions done well: *The Lion King*. As far as I'm concerned, it's the pièce de résistance of introductions.

We're introduced to the setting of Pride Rock with a broad lyrical rumination of how we are all very much connected, through an Elton John song, which, I think we can all agree, is the most obvious vehicle for a rumination like that.

And the central message of this lyrical sequence is thematically crucial. It's important that the viewer buy into this idea of connection and how circular the circle of life is, because all the animals in the movie already fully embrace this idea.

As the movie begins, we're introduced to all the animals traveling to Pride Rock where their lion king, Mufasa, lives with his royal family. Everyone is really feeling the celebratory vibe, and Rafiki, the shaman-monkey character, walks through the crowd and bear-hugs (monkey-hugs?) Mufasa like they are BFFs, despite probably not being naturally simpatico in the wild. I can't authoritatively say that monkeys and lions are adversaries in the wild, but if I had to guess, I would say that they probably aren't allies—final answer, Regis. But, because of Elton's song, we remember the circle of life thing, so it's fine. We go with it.

Next we realize the animals are celebrating the birth of Mufasa's son, Simba, the future king of Pride Rock. Here's where things get crazy: Rafiki presents Simba to the gathered animals and they *lose it*. These animals are for real acting like Oprah just gave them a car.

The monkeys act like they've freebased illegal stimulants, the antelopes are going bonkers supreme, and the giraffes literally *cannot even* with all of this lion-cub cuteness. These animals are handling this situation like white people would handle a 75-percent-off sale at Pottery Barn.[3]

We can all agree that this atmosphere is a little incredible, right? Rafiki is honoring the apex predator that feeds on all these animals (Mufasa) by presenting the next apex-predator legacy monster (Simba) who will not only feed on some of the very animals that are present, but also, probably, the children and grandchildren of those animals.

Imagine knowing that your current boss's son, no matter what, will eventually lord over you just because of "the circle of employment." Could you conjure up that kind of enthusiasm for your boss's son? I'm telling you right now that I super could not.

Anyway, the best part about this opening sequence is that, straight out of the gate, we get a sense of the royal hierarchy, the central players, and the primary character, Simba. Rafiki literally holds him up as a light shines on him.

Wouldn't life be better if all stories followed this template? You wouldn't have to trouble yourself with whether or not Duane from IT is someone you should spend time getting to know.

My point is, the best introductions tell you what is up concisely *and* creatively. You get a little bit of information with a side of entertainment. And truthfully, I just want a proper introduction and context on who I'm spending time with. Ever notice how some books jump right into things like we've been dropped into a noir crime novel?

"Gutshot and panicked, I arrived at the destination of my emotional abyss."

---

3. I say *would handle* because Pottery Barn never offers any kind of significant discount. They just make you stare down the reality that like it or not, you will pay $129 for a table runner and there's nothing you can do about it.

An opening line like this and I'm like, "Who is this gutshot person? And what abyss destination have we arrived at? Is it a Chuck E. Cheese? Or a *metaphorical* Chuck E. Cheese?"

Maybe I'm a simple man with simple desires, but I like to get to know someone before arriving at the destination of our emotional abysses together, you know what I mean?

For example, if we were meeting, I'd want to communicate the following in an effort to make a connection with you:

I am Knox, December-born, of the House McCoy, First of His Name Probably, Easily Burnt on Beaches, King of the Grill and the Barbecue Smoker and Allergic to Grass, Cats, and Shellfish, Breaker of Small Talk and Social Engagements at the Last Minute If at All Possible, and Father of Poorly Conceived Yet Ambitious Metaphors.

And now that we have that connection, you should probably also know that everything I know about life I learned in some part from *The Wonder Years*.

The theme song—Joe Cocker's cover of "With a Little Help from My Friends"—taught me the need for community.

The use of adult Kevin as younger Kevin's narrator made me aware that there might be an omniscient presence observing my life too. (Definitely God, but sometimes Santa too, and they probably compared notes.)

And remember how for a hot minute, everyone thought Josh Saviano, the actor who played Kevin's best friend Paul, grew up to be Marilyn Manson? That made me confront a reality in which the world of popular culture could fold neatly into the realm of spirituality and potential principalities of darkness.

As a kid, I spent a lot of time caught up in my own thoughts and chasing them around inside my head. I spent time parsing silly things like why Donkey Kong was called "donkey" when he was really a giant ape or how on earth Kevin Arnold could snag Winnie Cooper.

But I also tried deconstructing deeper questions, like who God was and what it was that he wanted from me. It was often pop culture that helped me fill in the gaps of my understanding— sometimes in hilarious ways, and sometimes in ways that were accidentally profound.

And that's what this book is about: how I navigated life in the time I call *the wondering years*.